D0394911

WHERE YOU
ARE IS NOT
WHO YOU ARE

A MEMOIR

URSULA M. BURNS

AMISTAD

An Imprint of HarperCollins*Publishers*

WHERE YOU ARE IS NOT WHO YOU ARE. Copyright © 2021 by Ursula M. Burns.
All rights reserved. Printed in the United States of America. No part of this
book may be used or reproduced in any manner whatsoever without written
permission except in the case of brief quotations embodied in critical articles
and reviews. For information, address HarperCollins Publishers, 195 Broadway,
New York, NY 10007.

HarperCollins books may be purchased for educational, business, or sales
promotional use. For information, please email the Special Markets Department
at SPsales@harpercollins.com.

FIRST EDITION

Designed by Terry McGrath

Library of Congress Cataloging-in-Publication Data has been applied for.

ISBN 978-0-06-287929-5

21 22 23 24 25   LSC   10 9 8 7 6 5 4 3 2 1

To
Olga Racquel Burns—my rock, a true superwoman
And
Lloyd Fitzgerald Stuart Bean—
my love, exactly who and what I needed
And
Malcolm Khalil Moore Bean and Melissa Racquel Bean—
the greatest gifts I have ever received

I am the one thing in life I can control
I am inimitable

—*Hamilton: An American Musical*

CONTENTS

PREFACE

I started writing this book well before the world as we knew it changed. Pre-pandemic and pre–social justice reawakening and pre–the end of the darkest four years in my life. I finally responded to the encouragements—"You have to write a book"—I received after speaking engagements and conversations. I must say that writing this book has been much, much harder than I thought it would be. Not only because of the before-and-after situation that we are still in the midst of, but also because it is hard for me to find a lot that is truly remarkable or book-worthy about my story. I am not being humble in that statement—the fact of the matter is that life happens one day at a time, and only in the retelling does it come together into remarkable, exciting, or insightful stories. In other words, you live your life not knowing the end of the story, and retell it only as if you knew what the outcome would be.

In this book I hope you see that good things can and do happen. I hope you see how much of a positive impact one person who is neither rich nor famous can have on the world. I hope you see that hard work, belief in yourself, and support by good people are the magic sauce.

As of this writing, the pandemic is still here, social justice is awakening, and post-Trump America is in inning number one, but I am optimistic about America and the world. As I love to say, the USA is not a zero-sum nation. I've seen over and over that it is not necessary for someone else to lose in order for me to win. Someone doesn't have to starve for me to eat; someone doesn't have to go without health care or an education for me to have them. America, the world is not playing a zero-sum game. I am optimistic.

LEAVE BEHIND MORE THAN YOU TAKE AWAY

There was a huge uproar in the press in July 2009 when I was appointed chief executive officer of Xerox: the headlines proclaimed that I was the first Black woman to lead a Fortune 500 company and that for the first time the CEO mantle had been passed from one woman, Anne Mulcahy, the outgoing CEO, to another. What a ridiculous way to make history. Though both headlines were factually correct, the press missed what was a unique story: How did this happen? How is it that the Xerox Corporation had two female CEOs, one after another? How did the Xerox Corporation produce the first African American woman CEO? That should have been the conversation, not these ridiculous stories proclaiming, "Oh my god, not one but two women" and "Oh my god, a Black woman made it." Was it truly so amazing to think a Black woman could lead a multibillion-dollar company? I had worked at Xerox for twenty-nine years by then. I had a strong track record. I was very well educated. I hadn't been plucked from a circus sideshow. I had earned the position.

In that instant, I joined the top five hundred business leaders in the United States out of a population of 306.8 million. That is 0.000163 percent of the total population. And the repercussions were immediate. I got congratulatory calls or emails from at least a hundred other CEOs and from high-profile African Americans. I heard from my good friend and mentor Vernon Jordan, the corporate titan and adviser to President Clinton, and from Ken Chenault, the chairman and CEO of American Express, on whose board I sat. I also received congratulations from many others I didn't know, like the civil rights leaders Al Sharpton and Jesse Jackson and the basketball legend Magic Johnson, himself the CEO of the $1 billion Magic Johnson Enterprises. I got phone calls from US senators and members of Congress, and practically every company and nonprofit in the country asked me to join their boards. How many commencement addresses was I asked to make? How many speaking engagements? How many media interviews? My teenage daughter, Melissa, was unimpressed. "The phone's for you," she told me that night. "I think it's a newspaper or something."

The enormous amount of attention continued for days. I was at our home in Rochester, a midsize city in upstate New York and the manufacturing and engineering headquarters for Xerox at that time. Everyone knew everyone else, so there were smiles and congratulations on the street and in the grocery store and in the dry cleaner's every time I left the house. There were paparazzi too. It was impossible for me to be unaffected. I'd made it. I'd arrived. I felt terrific but also apprehensive. I was not becoming the CEO of Apple. I was becoming the CEO of Xerox, which had gone through two or three near-death experiences by then. The company had to be led, to be managed, to be strengthened, and it was not going to be an easy ride. Xerox needed a lot of work, and I quickly returned to the company's nondescript executive headquarters in Norwalk, Connecticut.

There was no lavish suite of offices and anterooms waiting for me, no special floor with private dining rooms, no moving from floor A to a fancier floor B, as so many corporations offer their top executives. That was not the way it was at Xerox, and I liked that egalitarian modesty. I returned to my old office where I'd worked for two years as president of Xerox, kitty-corner to the office Anne had used as CEO. Both our offices were larger than the others in the unremarkable and inexpensive four-floor building Xerox rented as our corporate headquarters, and each had a perk—a private bathroom, one with a shower. There were very few other Xerox executives in that building. The majority of the company's leadership lived in the field. The head of research and development lived in Rochester, as did the executive who ran manufacturing. The sales executive for the United States lived in New York City, while his counterpart for sales in Europe lived in France.

We had hundreds of offices and buildings all over the world, which now, in the midst of the 2020 COVID-19 pandemic, seems redundant. One of the questions the pandemic has laid bare is whether we really need to come into an office all the time to do our work. Between Zoom and Skype and Webex and Facebook Live, among others, technology has advanced to the point of making virtual offices feasible for almost all employees. But in 2009, we were still working in centralized locations.

After Anne stepped down as chair, I shifted into the CEO's office and I asked my chief financial officer, Larry Zimmerman, to move into my old office so he would be closer to me. (There was no longer a company president. We only used that title when we were going through a transition, and that transition had been completed.) Larry was a seasoned executive whom Anne had hired from IBM years earlier. Larry was invaluable to me, older, wiser, very straightforward, and strong. He was a great business partner and asset for me as the new CEO, especially as we were in the process of acquiring a new business.

Another and far more important perk than my private bathroom and shower was the company plane, which saved hours and hours of travel time. I could fly to Washington for a meeting at eleven and be back in Norwalk for a four o'clock meeting. Traveling commercially was a very inefficient use of time. I remember the bad old days early in my career when my team and I had to fly often to Japan to work with our partner, Fuji Xerox, on the 5100 copier, our first joint project. The United flight route then was through Seattle-Tacoma Airport (Sea-Tac), where we too often got delayed for five hours or nine hours or even a whole day because of the freakin' fog and rain, throwing off the entire schedule in Japan. Sometimes, if the CEO or someone in senior management was going to Japan, we got to fly on the company plane, which made the thirteen-hour trip more bearable but had its own downside. When I became CEO, I rarely flew in our own plane to Japan because of an irrational fear that if the plane went down in the China Sea and it was only me and the pilots, the rescuers might not look as hard for survivors as they would if a big airliner went down.

Closer to home, security became an issue. Shortly after I became CEO, I got an extensive briefing from Jim Danylyshyn, the head of Xerox's security team. Basically, it was common sense. You're no longer the normal citizen nobody knows—be extra mindful when you walk in the street—don't wear exposed expensive jewelry or other displays of wealth. "We damn sure don't want to have to get a new CEO," Jim said. "We don't want the publicity of somebody kidnapping you or somebody stealing from you." His briefing did not alarm me. It was a rational response to the heightened visibility of all aspects of your life when you become the CEO of a Fortune 500 company.

And there was cause for concern. In 2003, the CEO of Sears, Eddie Lampert, was kidnapped from the garage of his Connecticut office and held for ransom in a Day's Inn for four days. (Luckily for him, his abductors weren't very professional. Lampert negotiated a $5 million ransom and convinced his kidnappers that he'd get them the money if they freed him. They did, and Lampert walked into the nearest police station.) An Exxon vice president was not so lucky in 1992. He was ambushed in the driveway of his home in New Jersey, shot in the arm, and left bound and gagged in a self-storage vault where he died four days later.

Xerox had had its own incidents. The president of a Xerox operation in Paris was shot and seriously wounded in the office by a disgruntled ex-employee in 1990, and seven employees were shot to death in Hawaii in 1999 by a fifteen-year colleague who suspected them of conspiring against him. I didn't have to go that far to understand some of the risks, though I wasn't particularly worried about my own safety.

I was assigned a security person, a wonderful man named Ivan

Rivera, who had provided security for Anne. Ivan, a retired NYC policeman, drove me to and from meetings in New York, flew with me domestically in the company plane, and arranged for security when I traveled overseas. When I was home, I chose to drive my own car from our house in New Canaan, Connecticut, to our offices in nearby Norwalk, unlike some CEOs who never went anywhere without their security. To the consternation of the Xerox board of directors, which took security very seriously, I also often walked home alone to my apartment in New York after functions in the city. I love walking in New York, and it was not unusual for someone to stop me and say, "You're Ursula Burns!" Thankfully, nothing bad ever happened.

Ivan and I spent a lot of time in the car together—a lot. I almost always sat in the front seat, not only to avoid motion sickness but also because I really enjoyed his company. We talked about everything—his children, my children, basketball games, songs. He was a colleague and friend, and we shared many of the same sentiments. I was in tears once when I called him to change a pickup time. "What's the matter?" he said, and when I told him I'd been watching the devastating news coverage of frightened and injured children in war-torn Aleppo and wanted somehow to get them out of Syria, he teared up too.

My promotion to CEO came at a perilous time for the US and global economy. The year 2009 saw the end of George W. Bush's administration and the beginning of Barack Obama's, an election that brought a lot of joy but occurred during the most dangerous economic time since the Great Depression. The country was slowly beginning to recover from the 2007–2008 global recession, which had been precipitated by excessive risk-taking by banks, the failure of the investment bank Lehman Brothers, and the imminent collapse of the auto industry. Detroit declared bankruptcy, the stock market tanked, and all over the country many people lost their jobs and homes. It was an unbelievably bad time for the economy and for every US company, including Xerox.

The US government was one of our largest customers, along with the banking and auto industry. Xerox faced a heightened risk of bankruptcy because those sectors were so strained that payments were delayed indefinitely. Xerox was primarily a business-to-business (B-to-B) company, which means that we sold to other businesses, unlike business-to-consumer (B-to-C) companies like Proctor & Gamble or Nestlé, which sell many of their products to end consumers. As the world economy slowed down, our business slowed down, everybody's business slowed down. Spending was tightened around the world, and optimism was low.

In retrospect, the economic crisis that started in 2007 and continued into 2010 is nothing compared to the financial catastrophe caused by the pandemic of 2020. Multiple countries shuttered businesses and did not allow them to operate, and rightly so. You could not manufacture anything; you could not leave your home to go to your office. The economic system, as we knew it, was literally put on stop—not hold. The earlier crisis was difficult, to be sure, but the pandemic has created financial challenges that make that time seem like child's play. As of this writing in October 2020, some countries are beginning to open up, but the long-term effect of the financial freeze is unknown.

When President Obama took office in January 2009, the impacts of the 2007–2008 financial crisis were still not fully known. To get better insight into how businesses were recovering and how the government could help, President Obama began holding small lunches at the White House for business CEOs. I was invited to one in June of that year. Though technically I was still president of Xerox and not yet the CEO, I was the heiress apparent. As part of my transition to CEO, Anne had asked me to stand in for her at several high-level meetings, and the White House lunch was one.

Because of Anne, I already knew quite a few CEOs, including my fellow lunch guests: Randall Stephenson, CEO of AT&T; Muhtar Kent, CEO of Coca-Cola; and Dave Cote, CEO of Honeywell. (I had spoken to the leadership team of Muhtar's company a few times, once on women's leadership.) They were all really good guys and successful leaders, and we became good friends. CEOs have lots in common even if they work in different industries: tax and regulation, trade, and immigration policies affect every industry. The companies represented at this White House lunch faced similar economic strain because of the fiscal crisis.

The unknown at the fifty-minute lunch in the president's private dining room was the president himself. I had met him once before his election but just to shake his hand. What was kind of amazing at the lunch was the immediate connection that I, and I think all of us, felt to him. He was serious, kind of casual, knowledgeable, and fun. And that's a good foundation on which to build a relationship.

Nothing earth-shattering came out of the brief meeting from a factual standpoint or a detailed action plan. It was instead an opportunity to listen to this brand-new president and feel one another out, like on a first date.

We turned out to be cheap dates. Demonstrating the president's seriousness regarding ethics and any conflict of interest, we got billed for the lunch! The government does not fund the business world, Obama pointed out to us, so when businesspeople came to eat at his place, he was not going to pay. I chuckled at that, but he was right. Why should the taxpayer pay for a meal we could definitely afford on our own? At least we got to eat. In a subsequent business meeting at the White House with the heads of the country's biggest banks, including Jamie Dimon from JPMorgan Chase and Lloyd Blankfein from Goldman Sachs, the CEOs were only served water!

The first time I'd met Obama was bittersweet. Vernon Jordan introduced me to him at a reception in New York in 2008 after Obama had defeated Hillary Clinton in the Democratic presidential primary. As much as candidate Obama was impressive and as much as I would support him in his bid for the presidency, I was a big supporter of Hillary. I had worked closely with her when she was the senator from New York and I was the head of the manufacturing and supply chain at Xerox. I had been truly impressed by Hillary's interest and her grasp of the most minute details of the business challenges Xerox was facing at the time, and she became a personal friend.

My Black friends were surprised by my primary choice. I was often asked, "You mean to tell me that you supported Hillary over Obama?"

I'd respond, "Why would that be surprising?"

"Because you're Black."

"Well, I'm also a woman."

I'm not surprised that people felt this way. In the Black hierarchy, Blacks are more coalesced around being Black than women are about being women. And there's good reason. People make up their mind about how they see you, and race is the defining attribute. If you're a Black American woman, you're seen first as Black, not as a woman, whereas if you are white, you're seen first as a woman.

Despite my early support for Hillary, I became a huge supporter of Barack Obama after the Democratic presidential nomination, and I was delighted to meet him again in the White House.

At the White House, I was struck by the access I had to the highest echelons of power by virtue of my pending title at Xerox. My upcoming job as the steward of an $8 billion company not only afforded me a seat at a private lunch with the president of the United States and with other CEOs, but also access to those who made public policy for the country.

Soon after I became CEO, I joined the Business Roundtable (BRT), a pro-business lobbying group made up solely of CEOs that meets regularly with government. We gathered three or four times a year in Washington, where the BRT rented three floors of a building near the Canadian embassy. The space was not glamorous. I was surprised the first time I went that we all sat on little folding chairs. The hundred or so of us who opted to join—some CEOs chose not to engage—were all on different committees representing business-related policy issues: education, finance, energy, infrastructure, and immigration.

The CEOs were a pleasant and quite informal group. We didn't have a special CEO handshake or badge. A number of issues naturally brought us together: the burdens of this or that tax, the longshoremen's strikes that tied up import and export at the harbors in California, the need to reach out for recommended people to fill board seats. We bonded over shared business concerns and spoke more or less the same language, but did I feel I belonged in the CEO club? Not really.

Part of it was that I was a woman and part because I was Black. I was one of a kind. But I also had a different background and different interests and spent time in different social circles. In short, when you look at the most common attributes and characteristics of a CEO, I had very few of them.

I didn't feel lesser, however. By that time, I was accustomed to not being part of the mainstream. It was just that I had not shared the life experiences of the other CEOs. Their conversations about summer homes in Kennebunkport or Nantucket or going hunting or on winter skiing trips to Jackson Hole or the Swiss Alps with their children and grandchildren were totally foreign to me. That was not where I was from.

My single mother and I had never taken a vacation. I'm not sure I even knew the word as a kid. From the age of fourteen, when I'd gotten my work papers, I had worked after school, every weekend, and every school holiday, mostly at the checkout counter at Woolworths or in special summer jobs created for poor inner-city kids. Skiing? What was that? Tennis? Really? Swimming? No way. I'm convinced that the colleges that require a swimming test for graduation created that requirement to keep poor kids from applying. And though I'd had the means for quite a while to do all the things the other CEOs were talking about, it didn't occur to me. I had no history of this type of behavior. My husband and I had created our own vacation patterns, like visiting cities in Europe or going to Bermuda, where he had family. I still don't know how to swim.

The biggest gap between me and the other CEOs was golf. I didn't golf. I had no interest in golf. It took hours out of the day when I'd much rather be with my family. But golf was a huge pastime with the CEOs, especially at Augusta National in Georgia, the site of the Masters golf tournament. Forget that Blacks weren't allowed in the club as members until 1990 and that women were barred until 2012, when Condoleezza Rice, George W. Bush's former secretary of state, and Darla Moore, a South Carolina financier, were invited in, followed by Ginni Rometty, the CEO of IBM, a major sponsor of the Masters. Augusta was paradise to golfers, including Vernon Jordan, who lives for golf and forgave all to play on its championship course. I remember expressing my amazement to Vernon and members of the Xerox board who were salivating over the prospect of golfing at Augusta. "How can you possibly want to go to this place to golf when a short time ago they wouldn't let you join?" I asked Vernon. He told me that it was a beautiful place, that it was iconic, and so on. It didn't matter a bit to me that Augusta had finally opened its doors. Even if I were a great golfer, I would not have gone.

Another divide between me and the other CEOs was our degrees. Many of them had gone to business or law school. I hadn't studied business or law. My undergraduate and graduate degrees are in engineering, making me one of the few CEOs who came up through the engineering track. Another CEO with a BS was Don Thompson, the CEO of McDonald's and one of only five African American men to lead a Fortune 500 company during my tenure. That's five Black male CEOs out of five hundred—0.01 percent! Women didn't fare much better. In my time, only sixty women in history had made it to CEO, starting with Katharine Graham, who assumed the leadership of the Washington Post Company in 1972. As of January 2018, according to *Forbes* magazine, twenty-seven women were CEOs of Fortune 500 companies—a whopping 5.4 percent—and that was a huge gain! But not one is Black. That distinction died with my retirement in 2017.

The corporate model is male—white male—and always has been. We all start out with two arms and two legs and a head, but if you're born white with testicles and a penis, you're already way ahead of the game. More than half of the world's population is female, but that certainly is not reflected in access to wealth, education, or power. Women are making progress in the political sphere, as shown by the record number of women (102) in Congress after the midterm elections in 2018, including thirty-five Black women, nine Latinas, two Muslims, and two Native Americans. Still, it's just a drop in the gender bucket. I read recently in the *New York Times* that there are more CEOs named John than there are CEOs who are women.

Many gender studies have examined why women are not near parity in high-level executive positions. Though women make up 52 percent of the professional workforce, the number in C-suite jobs is under 10 percent. Some studies cite women's reluctance to promote themselves, while others say women who do promote themselves are disliked by both men and women. This catch-22 is thought to be a large part of Hillary Clinton's failed bid for the US presidency in 2016. Though she would have been accepted as president, she was not accepted for having the ambition to run. A high percentage of suburban white women voted for Trump.

I have no real idea what people thought of me. There must have been some who looked at my "rapid" (if twenty-nine years can be rapid) career progression to CEO and muttered "Affirmative action" under their breath. So be it. If my race and gender worked for me instead of against me, I'll take it. I don't know what my fellow CEOs thought of me either, but I didn't care much. They were all universally polite and friendly enough, though at times our interactions were awkward. Not only did we have little shared experience save for business, but we shared no overlapping relationship circles. There I was, a woman who didn't look like their wives or their mothers, a woman who had shared little of their life experiences, so I was one, two, three circles removed. As a Black woman, I was not a natural fixture in their lives. I was totally and completely foreign to them, though they were much more familiar to me.

Many white people live their entire lives without having more than passing interactions with Black people, but it is impossible for Black people not to have continual interactions with white people. They are the cops, the government officials, the domestic employers, the bosses at work, the customers in the supermarkets being checked out by minorities. On the other hand, white people can avoid us easily. White people can get up in the morning, get in their cars, drop their kids off at school, drive to their jobs, pick their kids up, go to their country club, and never see a Black person except for the servers by the time they get home to their bubbles. Very few of us live in truly integrated communities. I call it the "ghettoization" of America. We have developed communities that are divided by color, by nationality, by income: rich, white ghettos, poor Native American ghettos, Chinese ghettos, Black ghettos, and on and on. The structure of American society is based on that compartmentalization. While white people can move through all these communities with impunity, the rest of us cannot move through theirs. Maybe the accepted structure will open up in three or five or seven generations, but for now, our entire lives as Black people and as women have been spent conforming to a structure built by white men on the backs of Black people and other minorities—a structure that we can't be completely a part of.

Different rules apply to different ghettos. The police that go into Black neighborhoods are heavily armed with guns, bullet-proof vests, billy clubs, mace. That is not the case in the affluent white suburbs in Connecticut or Westchester County. The police in Black neighborhoods practice what is called "social control" through intimidation and terror tactics. They are police states. The police in Greenwich, Connecticut, on the other hand, are seen by the white residents as friends who are there to help, the opposite of how they are viewed in Black neighborhoods. I saw the dynamic in my own community as a kid. We didn't run to the police and tell them our problems. They were not our friends.

Nor were they George Floyd's friends in Minneapolis. For almost nine long minutes, Officer Derek Chauvin, a nineteen-year veteran of the police force, knelt on Floyd's neck, even as Floyd called out that he couldn't breathe. According to media reports, Chauvin's three fellow officers did nothing to stop him. I believe their assumption was that the police have a right to treat this other human being this way because he is Black and has a propensity to be violent and needs to be controlled. Some in the gathering crowd called for Chauvin to get off Floyd's neck, pointing out he was already unresponsive. But that didn't happen. Instead, their protests fell on deaf ears and they watched as Floyd was abused and treated like an animal until he died.

I marched in London, where I live now, in the international

protests demanding justice and police reform following Floyd's murder. My son, Malcolm, marched in Palo Alto, California. "Watch it," I warned him. "Be very careful if you're approached by a police person. The police will see you as a dangerous, young, Black man." I knew the police in Northern California wouldn't see Malcolm as a graduate student at Stanford University with three degrees from MIT. They would only see him as a Black male with all the associated stereotypes. No white mother would have to give that same advice to her son.

I had lived in my personal racial ghetto for years as "the only" among my fellow students and my white colleagues. I was used to it and made it work to my advantage. Because I stuck out in a sea of white, everything I did garnered attention. And I did well. I excelled in college and graduate school. I did very well at Xerox. I had confidence based on performance. And I worked hard. That strong foundation enabled me to participate at the highest level of the white, privileged world, whatever anomaly I might have been. CEOs I hadn't met yet were taken aback when they saw me at the Business Roundtable. "Oh, you must be Ursula," the usual comment, was delivered with relief.

As members of the Business Roundtable, we had access to many top government leaders who came to us to discuss or present policy: members of Congress; senators like Mitch McConnell, then the Senate minority leader; Valerie Jarrett, a senior adviser to President Obama; and even the president himself on occasion. There was no limit to our access, especially for the members of the Executive Committee, the governing body of the BRT, which

I soon joined. We had meetings with administration leaders like Ron Kirk, the US trade representative; Penny Pritzker, the secretary of commerce; and John Kerry, the secretary of state. And we offered our own policy perspectives, not those that would benefit our individual companies, but those that would benefit the country as a whole—energy policy, intellectual property protection, small business support, to name just a few. We had ideas and theories about just about everything.

My areas of focus were education, trade, and immigration. I was keen on those issues—education because of the lack of advanced math and science in our schools, which left the US woefully behind the rest of the world; immigration because we needed to bring in skilled talent from abroad to make up for our lack of it at home. For years I'd worked on the specific visas that allow highly skilled workers to come to the US. We didn't have enough engineers at Xerox and needed to draw from China, India, and other countries. And it wasn't just Xerox. There was a dearth of homegrown engineers in every industry.

The K–12 public education system is failing not only in poor communities but also nationwide in preparing students for careers in math, science, and engineering. This failure is borne out every day vis-à-vis our standing in the world. There is resistance to teaching math and science among the schools—oh, science is not that important, math is too hard. Within one state are schools that do well and graduate 90 percent of students with some degree of proficiency in the right areas, while down the street are schools that graduate 40 percent with zero proficiency.

I was able to take my case directly to Washington after Xerox won the National Medal of Technology and Innovation in 2005 under George W. Bush. I was president of Xerox then, and Anne sent me to the White House with a group of Xerox scientists and engineers to accept the honor from the president. The award gave me a bully pulpit from which to extol the importance of science, technology, engineering, and mathematics (STEM) education in our schools, and afterward I was asked over and over to Washington to brief members of the government.

Joining the Executive Committee of the BRT multiplied the requests from the government for me to speak on subjects beyond STEM education, including immigration, trade, and gender equality. I was not alone. Andrew Liveris of Dow Chemical, Ginni Rometty of IBM, and Ken Chenault of American Express were also high on the government's call list, but in my case, anyway, it got out of hand for three reasons. I was a woman. I was Black. And I was the only Black woman CEO. If I'd accepted every request, I wouldn't have had time to do anything else. Sometimes I said no, but more often I agreed to speak on subjects that I was passionate about, like STEM.

And so it was that I said yes to President Obama when he asked me to lead his White House National Program on STEM education in November 2009, along with Craig Barrett, former CEO of Intel; Glenn Britt, CEO of Time Warner Cable; Sally Ride, former astronaut and CEO of Sally Ride Science; and Rex Tillerson, CEO of Exxon Mobil. Obama and his administration had circled around a couple of priorities for his presidency. One was transparency. Another, he told us, was enabling more people to participate in the American dream.

The road to get there had changed. Historically, the American model for success had been to graduate high school, get a job, improve your skills, and parlay that foundation into a career and a good living for you and your family. That had been the path for white America, particularly white male America, during the Industrial Revolution.

The currency of today's world was very different from the currency of the previous generation, the president mused during our many conversations. Manufacturing, though it still existed, had been significantly devalued. The current currency was information and technology, and the new economies were exploiting the skill sets grounded in STEM. How could we boost these skills among the fastest growing portions of the population—underserved minorities and women—the president asked. And how come those groups didn't participate at anywhere near the same rate of white males? The core issue was education or, more accurately, the lack thereof.

The members of the STEM task force didn't just sit around and think about these questions. We gathered facts and data, like the shocking reality that American students ranked twenty-ninth in math and twenty-second in science compared to other students in industrialized countries. And it was not the students' fault. Too many schools did not offer the full range of math and science courses (algebra I and II, calculus, geometry, biology, chemistry, and physics), and those that did were schools with predominantly white and Asian American students. Far fewer schools with Black and Latino majority student populations offered STEM education. The inequality came down to zip codes.

The repercussions of this neglect were more than an example of racial bias. The lack of STEM education for lower-income and minority students blocked a potential pathway to prosperity. When

I started working with the president on STEM education, there were 150,000 unfilled jobs in the fields of science and mathematics in the US, with an average salary of $70,000!

Young white women were not contenders for these jobs either, but for different reasons. Many people saw math and science as "male" subjects, and girls who had done well in math started opting out around the eighth grade. At many high schools, girls were discouraged from entering the science track. Instead, they were directed to social sciences and the arts. One of the challenges of the STEM task force was determining how to motivate girls to take the science path. Role models, encouragement, and early involvement in STEM helped.

We also faced the question of how to prepare the schools in minority neighborhoods to hire the teachers and gather the books and tools to educate all their students across the board. It was a tricky endeavor. The federal government does not set school policy. The states do, which greatly enlarged our theater of operation. We came up with Change the Equation, an initiative that was supported by at least a hundred CEOs from the BRT in different states. The number of participating CEOs was amazing, but the prospect of a more highly skilled workforce was a motivating factor, and everyone wanted to help President Obama in this endeavor. Coalitions were formed. Private money flowed to train teachers in STEM education. Foundations, universities, and nonprofits signed on. STEM moved from a narrow academic discipline to the consciousness of the country.

Corporations were a force for positive social change in education at the time. It was to some extent self-serving in that a skilled workforce would benefit them, but corporate involvement was more altruistic than that. Corporate leaders recognized that the high-paying jobs were in STEM, so they unified around the idea of training more people in that area.

I see a parallel to the social justice movement today. While corporations continue to be focused on education, corporate leaders have also recognized their responsibility to contribute positively to societal change in the aftermath of George Floyd's murder and the ongoing pandemic. Companies like Pepsi-Cola and Walmart have pledged millions to fund social justice causes like Black Lives Matter. Companies have also started to be a lot more interested in listening to their employees and ensuring their safety. Amazon had to literally slow down its operations when its employees said, "Wait a minute. I don't feel protected from COVID." Corporations today are becoming positive drivers for societal change as they were for STEM education nine years ago.

Corporations are an integral part of society. Big companies employ millions of people, and to say that companies have no influence over the structure of the society that their employees live in is a folly. I am optimistic today because I see companies actively participating in social debates. In the past, businesses were reluctant to get involved in women's rights or climate change, for example, for fear of disenfranchising some employees, alienating customers, or ending up on the wrong side of a government official. Businesses today are recognizing that they can and should play an active role in defining, enabling, and ensuring a just and healthy society.

We were fortunate during the STEM task force days to have the Obama administration solidly behind us. We met often with Arne Duncan, the secretary of education, and almost as often with

President Obama at the White House to tell him what we'd found out, present our recommendations, and highlight programs. The president was hands-on. His investment in raising the educational level for all Americans was heartfelt, especially in math and science.

Common Core was introduced while we were working on STEM awareness, and all hell broke loose. Common Core did not offer a specific curriculum but a new and progressive way of teaching and evaluating students' progress. Instead of students being graded solely on correct answers to math problems, Common Core raised the standard and required that their work sheets be evaluated to show how they had come up with the answer. Similarly, in English, instead of a student being asked simple comprehension questions after reading an assigned story ("What color was the fairy's cloak?"), Common Core required more thoughtful questions ("What was the fairy's role in the story?") The move toward critical thinking skills and away from rote learning was aimed at making our kids competitive globally and ensuring they would be ready for the job needs of the future.

The STEM task force was a great champion of Common Core, but we faced an immediate, unbelievable, and shocking pushback from parents and state school officials, particularly in the south. The new standard called for a readjustment of what "good" looked like. An average student scoring 73 on a math test might receive a failing grade, and no parent or school wanted that. We faced a chorus of protests: "We cannot expect our children to perform at this level!" "What makes you think this is really needed?" "Who are you to call for these radical changes?"

Our requests fell on deaf ears. The members of Change the Equation pleaded with the boards of education in many states: "We travel around the world and we see how our children are doing in math and science compared to children in Estonia, Russia, Malta, Slovakia—you name the country—and our kids are way behind in these areas." Nothing. We pushed the states hard to implement Common Core, but they came back with all kinds of excuses and reasons why it was killing their children. The effort to get Common Core adopted just didn't work and was finally abandoned.

No one seemed to care that we were undereducating our children and not preparing them for the demands of the future. While our colleges and universities are second to none and draw students from all over the world, our K–12 educational system is really poor. Admitting defeat was hard, but no one could doubt our efforts.

I was appointed vice chair of the President's Export Council in March 2010, and then chair in 2015. The Export Council, which acts as a national advisory committee on international trade, was a big deal. There were at least twenty other business leaders on the council, including Jim McNerney, CEO of Boeing and the chair of the council, Bob Iger, CEO of the Walt Disney Company, and Denise Morrison, CEO of Campbell Soup Company, as well as eight senior members of the House and Senate and many officials in the Obama administration, including most of his cabinet. We served "at the pleasure of the president" and had to be vetted before being officially appointed. I was even given a title: The Honorable Ursula Burns. Amazing.

The work of the Export Council was very important to the American economy. Our mission was to identify ways to increase

US exports to other countries, like farm goods, small business trade, and tourism, among many others. Why is that a big deal? America was then a country of 300 million people, and we had a high standard of living based largely on our exports to the seven billion people in the rest of the world. The formula is simple—300 million versus a customer base of seven billion! Trade and trade access had always been vitally important interests of mine, and I enjoyed the work, though there was a lot of it.

The council was divided into smaller groups, and our job was to develop recommendations and then push the government to adopt our proposals. Tourism is one of the biggest contributors to this country's gross domestic product (GDP), and we worked hard to increase it. An early recommendation letter on travel and tourism, for example, proposed continued marketing of America as a tourist destination for international travelers; increasing tourism to the US by shortening the time our foreign consulates took to issue visas; expanding the Global Entry and TSA PreCheck programs; and improving our road and airport infrastructures, including passenger transit to and from our airports and seaports in gateway cities. Some of our airports, like LaGuardia and Kennedy, were so old and dilapidated that some international travelers avoided them. In fact, Joe Biden once compared La Guardia to a "third-world country." Both New York airports are now being overhauled and modernized.

I was seated next to the president at many Export Council meetings—positioned between him and the secretary of state, between him and the chief of staff, between him and the secretary of labor, and so on. That access to the highest levels of government was daunting at first but quickly became routine. The issue was always how to increase trade.

I was often called upon to answer questions about our recommendations from members of Congress or other government officials, and I was asked about the effects of specific policy on Xerox. I had excellent help from Michele Cahn Peters, our government liaison at Xerox. I usually spoke to groups without notes and was pretty good at that, but speaking to the government or giving testimony required a different type of preparation. Government officials often had very specific items they wanted me to cover, and Michele and I would prepare talking points. The ten points or so I'd been asked to respond to were going to be read into the record, so I couldn't do six of them in a normal freewheeling conversation. I had to fill in all the blanks formally.

The Export Council also traveled on occasion to bolster trade with the US. In September 2014, I led a high-level delegation on a commercial diplomacy mission to Poland and Turkey. There were a lot of us, including Arne Sorenson, CEO of Marriott, other CEOs and members of the Export Council, staff people, trade experts, and members of NGOs. We were accompanied by Secretary of Commerce Penny Pritzker; Stefan Selig, the undersecretary for international trade; Wanda Felton, the vice chair of the Import-Export Bank; and Scott Nathan, a special representative of the US Department of State. All in all, it was an impressive showing.

Poland was one of the twenty-five largest economies in the world at the time, yet it ranked fifty-fourth among US trading partners. This trip was meant to help close the gap. We included Turkey to follow up on President Obama's successful visit five years before, during which he'd pledged to elevate our bilateral commercial relationship. Our trip coincided with a heady moment in Poland—Prime Minister Donald Tusk had just been elected president of the European Union—and an even headier one in Turkey, where the Turkish people had just participated in the country's first popular election for president.

It was an exhausting four-day trip with back-to-back meetings from breakfast on with local entrepreneurs, business leaders, and government officials in each county, including President Recep Tayyip Erdoğan in Turkey. We had a US government plane to ferry us around, which helped with our collective fatigue. The mission was fruitful.

Less exhausting and much more fun was a historic three-day fact-finding visit to Cuba with the president and his family in March 2016. No American president had been to Cuba since Calvin Coolidge in 1928! Cuba had continued to be a prosperous site for US companies until the 1959 communist revolution led by Fidel Castro and was then vilified for nationalizing US properties and declared a terrorist state by the United States. The US government had imposed draconian sanctions against Cuba in 1962 and essentially closed it off to Americans. While Europeans had free access to Cuba, no Americans had been allowed to do business with Cuba or even go on their own to the island, which is just ninety miles off the coast of Florida.

Until President Obama's visit, that is. Secret negotiations between the US and Cuba brokered by Pope Francis in 2014 resulted in what became known as the "Cuban thaw." The trade embargo was eased, the bans against financial transactions and travel to the controversial island were lifted, Cuba was taken off the US list as a state sponsor of terrorism, and diplomatic relations were reestablished, which promised to reopen embassies in Washington and Havana.

I was among the many Americans who applauded the "thaw." The long-standing dysfunctional relationship between our two countries reminded me of cousins who had not spoken to each other for almost fifty years. Enough was enough. The impasse between the United States and Cuba was so old that a lot of Americans couldn't even remember what started the schism.

Our three-day trip to Cuba in March 2016 was one of the most memorable of my life. The challenge was to figure out a way to rebuild a connection between a twenty-first-century county, the United States, and a country that was still mired in the early twentieth century, Cuba. How do you do that? Our delegation tried to find an answer.

Most of our delegation was composed of government personnel, including John Kerry, Penny Pritzker, and other cabinet officials and members of Congress. There were only two of us from the President's Export Council: Arne Sorenson, the vice chair, and me. We brought along Michele Cahn Peters, Xerox's government affairs lead, and her counterpart from Marriott. The four of us flew down on a chartered plane, a Gulfstream G550, but the plane was not allowed to stay on the island for the three days we were there.

Our goal was to see if we could start discussions about establishing a supply chain hub in Cuba. The island was located conveniently as a stopover for ships bringing parts from point A to point B to eventually be distributed in the US. Establishing the hub would have been good for Cuba and good for us. During the deep-freeze between the US and Cuba, Florida had become the supply chain hub, resulting in overcrowded ports and docks and a lot of headaches.

Mostly, however, the trip was just plain fun. I'll never forget the rapturous crowds lining the streets of Havana and hanging out of apartment windows as we followed the president's car in a motorcade. There were a lot of Black people in Cuba at the bottom of the social and employment ladder, and they were ecstatic seeing our Black president go by. He was a god in their eyes, and they danced and waved flags and sang "We love Obama." It was like traveling with a rock star.

The trip was amazing for me personally. Imagine my going to a country that's largely Black, with a president who is Black, and being literally one of the first businesspeople to enter the forbidden country on an official business trip in fifty years! In addition, my mother's family is from Panama, and we share the same gene pool as the Hispanic Black countries in the northern part of Central America, including Guatemala, Honduras, and El Salvador. We were all part of the African Diaspora that populated Central, Latin, and North America. These were my people.

We had some great, relaxed dinners with the president, one at a famous *paladar*, a home restaurant in Cuba. The American delegation and some Cuban officials ate downstairs, while the president ate upstairs with Michelle and their daughters, Sasha and Malia. He came down to join us after dessert, pulled up a chair, and just hung out for a while. Hanging in frames on the wall were really old newspaper stories from before the '59 revolution, and the president regaled us with stories about them. One photo was of an old cigar factory, and it turned out the president knew all about Cuban cigars. Tobacco had been a crop in Cuba for hundreds of years, and the country's legendary hand-rolled cigars stemmed from the early sixteenth century. Such arcane knowledge was typical of the president.

John Kerry was with us at that dinner. He had great stamina. He could go late into the night with a cigar and a glass of whatever liquor he drinks. We tried to get the president to drink some rum and smoke a cigar, but he refused. He was working hard.

The president met for two hours with Cuban dissidents, including Berta Soler, the leader of the brave Ladies in White who conducted weekly demonstrations in Havana and whose members had been arrested by the dozens hours before President Obama arrived in Cuba. He referred to them and other dissidents in a fiery speech at the Gran Teatro, which was attended by President Raúl Castro. Obama advised Castro that he "need not fear the different voices of the Cuban people and their capacity to assemble and speak and vote for their leaders." I felt proud listening to him in that massive hall and again later when he answered a Cuban official who criticized the US for violence against Black minorities by saying, "At least we are a country that talks about our problems openly."

Sadly, soon after taking office in 2017, Donald Trump reversed most of President Obama's progress in establishing a new relationship with Cuba. Trump tightened the sanctions against Cuba that Obama had eased, made travel to Cuba virtually impossible for Americans, and increased restrictions against any financial transactions. Our project of establishing a supply chain hub in Cuba was dead in the water.

I felt blessed as a CEO to have access to Obama as my president. All CEOs are called on to help or advise their current administration at some point. Anne Mulcahy, for example, had had a working relationship with George W. Bush, which I would have honored but found ideologically difficult. I had no such reservations about President Obama. We were both Democrats, for starters, and while we might have had differing opinions at times, there were no social ideological differences, zero at the highest level.

From time to time, we, the CEOs and the president, had almost existential debates, asking "What does American democracy stand for?" His call for transparency sparked another debate. "Would you allow cameras and tape recorders into the deliberation rooms of the Supreme Court?" "Shouldn't the public be privy to the deliberations of the justices?" The discourse was not about the answer, but rather about how you think through an issue, how you balance the differing opinions, and how you get to a decision. The president was a true intellect. He had a great way of listening to others, analyzing and coalescing their opinions, and he was an amazing guy to be around.

Was I a close friend of his? Not really. That distinction belonged to the "Obama people," his old friends and colleagues from Chicago, some of whom, like Arne Duncan, Rahm Emanuel, Valerie Jarrett, and David Axelrod, served in his administration. I was, however, invited to a few White House parties that were not attached to any cause, and my husband, Lloyd Bean, and I went. It felt like being invited by friends to their house, and we had so much fun. I met Michelle Obama for the first time on a purely social basis, and we all just hung out, dancing and chatting. Those evenings were magical.

It was my very good fortune to have become CEO at almost the same time Obama took office, and we remained in our positions during the same period. There had never been a US president who looked like him, nor a Fortune 500 CEO who looked like me. There was nothing phony about him—and that, among so many posturers in the government and business, was very refreshing.

I could have turned down all these extracurricular activities and concentrated solely on running Xerox, but I didn't. Instead, I added them to what was an already overfull life. I accepted almost every invitation to speak at schools and colleges about the importance of STEM and engineering as a career for young women. (I wanted them to see me as a wife and mother, and while not exactly hip, at least not a nerd.) I accepted invitations to speak at other companies about gender equality and leadership and the need for diversity, and I delivered the commencement address at several colleges, including Olin, the University of Rochester, and MIT. I even spoke to the CIA at the request of Vernon Jordan, who was a member of the CIA External Advisory Board.

My mother had a lot of crazy sayings she drummed into me and my siblings as kids. One was "Leave behind more than you take away," and that's what I tried to do by serving seven years on the president's STEM task force, six years on his Export Council, and all my CEO years on the Business Roundtable. It was a form of patriotism, to give back to the country that had made so much possible for me. Her lesson was similar to the familiar biblical quotation "To whom much is given, much is required," and I tried to live up to it—all the while doing my day job as CEO of Xerox.

DON'T LET THEM
SEE YOU SWEAT

The dinner for four in Dallas cost Xerox $6.3 billion and was extraordinary. The guest of honor was Lynn Blodgett, CEO of Affiliated Computer Services (ACS). Dining with Lynn were Larry Zimmerman, Xerox's CFO; Anne Mulcahy, the outgoing CEO of Xerox and board chair; and me, the incoming CEO. On the table was the potential purchase of Blodgett's company, which would allow Xerox to transform itself from the business machines company that had defined photocopying for decades into a provider in the newer, lucrative world of business services.

We had to diversify for Xerox to grow. While growth in and of itself is not the most important thing for a company or a CEO, it is one of the top three, along with profitability and a winning strategy. Without revenue growth, profits would shrink because a company's cost of doing business stays the same or increases, particularly a company with great labor costs. The cost of living goes up. People expect and deserve raises. The cycle requires that your top line grows at about the same rate as your costs, at least at the rate of inflation. To keep balance in a company, growth is important, and this was especially true when I was about to take over Xerox.

Xerox was operating in an industry with built-in technology-driven irrelevance. For all the brilliance of our machines, the move to digital picture frames and devices like smartphones reduced the need to print photographs and documents. We still generated $2 billion in cash annually, but looking down the road the traditional market for Xerox would continue to shrink without diversifying. That's why we were having dinner with Lynn Blodgett.

Anne and I were meeting Lynn for the first time. Larry already knew him, having spent months getting us to this point. It would be a huge deal for Xerox if we could work out at least an understanding with Lynn on the path forward. The two small business services companies we already owned—one in legal services, the other in mortgage services—were a good start in our strategy to diversify, but it would take years of similar small acquisitions to reach the desired size, and here was ACS, an established and profitable company in business process outsourcing that already had most of what we wanted.

Companies were already embracing business process outsourcing in areas such as information technology, payroll services, security services, and processes like legal discovery. ACS was the only company that had different business processing capabilities under one roof. If we could work out a deal with Lynn, Xerox would be positioned for the future.

Conversely, we had what Lynn wanted: the Xerox brand, which

meant reliable, innovative quality and service, along with a set of technologies that ACS could apply to their business to increase efficiency. And Xerox could help ACS expand its reach around the globe, which would be good for the US-centered company. We chatted at dinner about our two companies and whether we would be a good match. He was sizing us up, and we were sizing him up. It wasn't necessary that we "love" him, but it would have been really difficult if we didn't like him at all. In business terms, "love" and "like" are about the cultural fit. "Love" would require that Lynn have the same goals we had, the same moral approach, the same lingo, and the same company culture and also be brilliant and successful at business. "Like" would mean that there might be a couple of things that are not exactly ideal, but none of the important things. As dinner progressed, Anne and I decided we both liked Lynn a lot. He was important to the deal, and we wanted him to stick around for the first twelve to eighteen months at a minimum. Was he willing?

We had a green light from Lynn by the time we got to coffee. Anne and I felt that this consolidation was something that could work, that it was worth going forward. We both knew it would require a significant but manageable effort, and we were willing to accept the risks inherent in buying an already running entity. One risk arises from merging employees from various new geographical locations. Another is the potential hidden bombs you might find in the company. As much as you spend on due diligence, until you own the company you never know all the details. The seller, quite naturally, has only shown you the best. The third risk is what is called "change of control" provisions. Both of our companies had signed contracts with many clients, and Xerox would have to get agreements from as many ACS clients as possible before closing. And the risks don't stop there. Some shareholders won't want the purchase to go through. Some shareholders will think you paid too much, while the other side will think you paid too little. And then there's the government, which might want you to sell a division or two for anti-monopoly reasons. The road ahead had many potholes. Still, I was very excited about the consolidation, though wary about the amount of work it would take to be successful. I was right.

The project kicked off at the same time I became CEO and was a huge distraction to what would have been the normal first six months of a new CEO. Instead of holding town halls with Xerox employees or visiting customers or working with my team or cleaning up the ramifications of my physical move, I basically handed the day-to-day operations over to my management team while I worked with Larry Zimmerman and our general counsel, Don Liu, on the details of the still-secret negotiation with ACS. We wanted to sew it up before the business community caught wind of it, which ended up requiring two months of daily, hourly, minute-by-minute phone calls and meetings on weekdays, weekends, early mornings, and late nights.

Most calls regarded financial issues, but other issues presented themselves: whether ACS could keep their plane, whether we were going to assume more of ACS's debts, whether we were going to leave individuals in certain positions. One challenge was negotiating with Darwin Deason, a major stockholder and the company's founder. He owned preferred stock, which entitled him to special voting rights. He owned 25 percent of the ACS shares, but every one of his shares could vote twice in any decision. ACS also provided him with certain services, like his own plane, which we would have to buy out or accommodate.

At times, accusations of broken commitments from both sides led to consideration of calling off the whole deal. At other points, we were really close to an agreement but then Don would call and say, "We're in a pens-down moment." I remember a short family holiday in Bermuda being interrupted by a call from Larry. I was pacing up and down on the beach talking to him when the line suddenly went dead. My phone had died from perspiration, but only temporarily, thank goodness.

The drama continued until we finally struck a deal with ACS in September 2009, two months after I had become CEO, and both our boards approved it. We scheduled the public announcement for Tuesday, September 29, at eight in the morning, followed by press interviews at nine, but then we heard from sources that somebody, probably a banker, had leaked the story to the press. This was bad news. We didn't want Xerox stock to be traded before the news of the ACS purchase was made available to the general shareholders. We had an emergency conference call and hurriedly moved up the date to September 28, which created another problem. I did not realize that the 28th was the Jewish religious holiday of Yom Kippur, and Xerox was roundly criticized for disrespecting the holiday. I felt terrible about it and apologized on the many press calls that morning, but there was nothing we could do. And the next round of negotiations began, this time with our major shareholders who had yet to vote on the acquisition of ACS.

I met with Marvin Schwartz in the maze of offices at Neuberger Berman, the famous New York investment company that was a major shareholder in Xerox, and it was intense. He is very smart, with an extraordinary and long track record of value investing. He does extensive homework for his clients and invests for the long term. He looks at a company's management team, financial structure, and business model, and if all seems healthy, he advises his clients to invest. Though smart and tough, he was also an old curmudgeon. I'd met him a couple of times while I was president of Xerox, but here I was as the brand-new CEO pitching the acquisition of ACS. He was a bit taken aback at first, but he quickly got into it: "Explain this to me. Give me the numbers. Prove to me this is a good idea." In other words, "Sell it to me."

Larry was with me and gave his pitch about the financial potential of the combined businesses, and I gave mine regarding the potential for additional services that could be created by increasing ACS's global reach and raising the ACS offering by applying Xerox's world-renowned research and development, strong brand, and excellent reputation.

Selling a deal can be a show—it's not just about the numbers but also about you and your confidence in the deal. But in the case of Neuberger Berman, they couldn't have cared less about how passionate or impressive I was. They'd been through presentations like ours a thousand times. The long-term investors just wanted to see the numbers and ask fifty questions—"Have you thought about this?" "Have you thought about that?"

I don't know whether we got their vote or that of another major investor who already owned stock in both Xerox and ACS. What I do know is that in February 2010, 96 percent of Xerox shareholders voted in favor of the acquisition, along with 86 percent of ACS shareholders. With that, ACS became Xerox Business

Services, our total market opportunity rose to $500 billion, and our employee base grew to 130,000.

We were thrilled, and in typical Xerox style, our celebrations were team based: picnics, congratulatory communications, a few dinners for special contributors. Xerox was not a company that went overboard in any way. We didn't give cruises to the best players or cars or gold watches. The special recognition awards we had for people who had done singular work were modest in comparison to the traditional dollar amounts handed out by banks.

The nine months of my life that I spent on the ACS deal were incredibly challenging. There was no downtime. The amount of time I had to do anything other than flying somewhere, reading, dealing with calls, going through the papers, looking at financials, making decisions about legal entities and taxes, and going through rehearsal sessions was very, very limited. There was not a moment I wasn't totally consumed by the project. I slept with the phone by my bed in case problems emerged from different time zones.

Life was slightly easier after the acquisition, but I was just as consumed by my work as CEO as I had been as president and even in my senior executive jobs. I worked every minute for Xerox whether I was in the office or not, reading and answering emails, talking on the phone, prepping for meetings, and initiating calls with employees who had problems, investors, board members, customers. Other than working, I slept and I ate. But even when I ate, I was available and often engrossed in the Xerox world. This was unhealthy for me and definitely for my family. When I engaged with my family on Saturday mornings, I was always semi-distracted, so I changed course.

From Saturday noon on, I didn't allow the noise of Xerox to

drown out my life. I didn't do anything special. I'd go food shopping or hang out at home with my husband and kids, maybe watch football, listen to music, or just zone out. Sometimes I would do my daughter's hair. Melissa has amazingly beautiful, thick hair, and Lloyd and I had to wash it and braid it because when she was younger she couldn't take care of it on her own. I reserved my weekends for doing nothing in particular. And then the Xerox week would start again at about eight on Sunday evening.

I couldn't have seen it through without the support of my husband, who had retired from Xerox some years before to take care of the kids and run the household. In fact, in my many talks to young women while I was at Xerox, I advised them to follow my lead and marry older men—Lloyd was twenty years my senior—so if they married and had children, they could work undistracted and worry-free.

New CEOs have to introduce themselves to a company and set the tone for the future, and I was no different. Granted, most people in the company already knew me or certainly had heard of me. I'd been around Xerox for twenty-nine years by the time I became CEO, but they didn't know what I expected of them or how I'd lead the company. So there was great curiosity when I finally surfaced from the ACS consolidation marathon and convened the annual Xerox get-together of our sales reps in Orlando, Florida.

Eyebrows must have shot up during my remarks to the hundreds of Xeroxers gathered in February when I admonished them not to be so nice to each other! "The Xerox family suffers from 'terminal niceness,'" I said to them. My basic message was that we had such an overly kind culture at Xerox that we at times supported each other's mediocrity. "When someone makes a presentation at a meeting and it's horrible, we actually say, 'Thank you. It was very good.' And when the person leaves, we say to each other, 'That was the worst presentation ever!' We've got to get over that and speak up." A simple example of a complex problem.

I have always been blunt in expressing my opinions, sometimes with good results, sometimes not. But it always stimulates discussion and saves time. My point was that we all had to be a little brusquer and risk disagreeing with each other so that we could get through the problems faster and speak about them in a comfortable way without having to mince words. It was such a waste of time to be overly polite. What I was proposing was that it was more than okay to be a bit more confrontational around issues we shouldn't compromise on in order to get everyone's ideas on the table. The goal was not to fight or scream or throw things, but to engage in hard conversations.

I practiced what I preached throughout my tenure as CEO. The role of a leader, I'd picked up some years ago from my friend and mentor Ken Chenault, is to define reality and give hope. Those words were my mantra, especially the definition of reality. I was never one of those blowhards who blithely proclaim everything is all right. I was very clear—we're spending too much money here, or we did great here but not so great there.

For example, Xerox was well known for its great research and development. Our Palo Alto Research Center (PARC) was known worldwide for its ingenuity and inventions, including the roots of the personal computer and the mouse, which Steve Jobs capitalized on at Apple. The specialized training of salespeople at our

Leesburg Training Center in Virginia was also well known. We developed a set of methods and trained the best salespeople not only for Xerox but, it turned out, for their future careers. Salespeople move around, and our training positioned them to move up the business ladder wherever they worked. Another of our strengths was manufacturing. We made the best, sturdiest machines in the world. They would last twenty-five years, which is great and a subject of pride, but when times change, that sturdiness becomes an albatross.

Our business, like any business, had to take our strengths and adapt them to meet the needs of current customers and current markets, and that responsibility fell to me as CEO. I had to take our strengths in R&D, selling, and manufacturing and use those attributes as a foundation to change the company without trashing the company's past.

Change is always a hard sell, but we were missing some of the trends, and change was necessary. Xerox was well known for its research capabilities, but it did not always yield outputs that Xerox could use, and the activities could take significant time to mature. Some companies were replacing or augmenting their internal R&D by acquiring smaller start-up companies or partnering with universities. Selling was moving from face-to-face sales to internet selling and marketing or selling though resellers. Finally, product life cycles were getting shorter, with new generations with more functionality coming to market faster and faster. We had to shift from our largely go-it-alone R&D, our lengthy direct selling, and our product design and manufacturing of tank-like equipment. We had to adjust everything we were known for.

I got quite a lot of blowback for my tough-love approach from those who would have preferred a cheerleader instead of a critic. They were taken aback by my frankness about what we didn't do well. I countered, when possible, by pointing out our strengths. My style was very different from Anne's. A former salesperson, she had been really good at cheerleading and motivational speaking, whereas my motivational speaking was often about where I wanted us to improve. Anne's approach worked very well for her, but I just couldn't do what she did. As close as we were, our personalities were very different.

"Don't let them see you sweat" was one of Anne's theories about leadership, an idea she'd probably inherited from Paul Allaire, her predecessor. My approach, largely restricted to the leadership team, was to let them see me sweat. I had to let my team see me when I was not so definitive, when I didn't have an area all locked up, so they could fill in the gaps. It was crucial to the other eight members of the management team who ran the company and were responsible for most of the high-impact decisions we had to make. We, as a team, made up the whole. I, alone, had a ton of blind spots.

I didn't pretend to know everything, and I relied on the expert members of my team to recognize when I felt unsure, especially Darrell Ford, the chief human resources officer; Christa Carone, head of marketing; Don Liu, general counsel; and Kathy Mikells, who had replaced Larry Zimmerman as CFO after he retired. We knew each other well, and I wanted them to speak up and say, "Ursula, I've got this," either to help me out personally—"I understand your husband is sick"—or professionally—"The legal aspects of this are in my field. I'll explain them to you, but let's go together and I'll be the leader on this." I appreciated this assistance. I felt very comfortable not being the smartest person in the room.

In presentations to customers or our own employees or another CEO, I felt relaxed asking the members of my team to lend their expert voices. Don Liu, for example, was brilliant on diversity. As part of a first-generation Asian American family, Don had to live through a particular set of stereotypes. He was very smart and hardworking, which fit the Asian stereotype, but unlike the accepted categorization, he did not want to remain anonymous behind the scenes making others look good. He wanted to be general counsel and not just, say, a legal expert on intellectual property. He'd run up against prejudice in a former company. "You don't look the part of general counsel," they told him. "You're a Korean guy, and we need an American guy." He'd joined Xerox as general counsel, and he was invaluable to me not only in our diversity presentations to other companies but also in tackling the bias against the minority groups at Xerox—women, Blacks, and Hispanics.

Reliance on others had been very hard for me at first. I am not naturally a group person. In high school and even college, I didn't join extracurricular activities like the yearbook or the softball team. I didn't belong to any organizations. Though more often than not my schoolmates wanted me to be engaged, I was generally uninterested in the crazy little things they did. I had friends, but I kept my own counsel and was comfortable acting independently.

My transition to teamwork happened gradually and surprised me to a degree. It started with my lab technician, Dick Schiek, in my early years as an engineer. Whereas I was good at theory, he was really good at practice. Ours was a small partnership, just him and me in a lab, but I was pleased at how much better I was with this guy next to me. My confidence in others grew slowly as I rose rapidly up the ladder in the organization, from an engineer to an engineering manager to a team leader in a very short time, but I didn't often mix socially with my coworkers. I had my personal life, and I had my work life, and I kept them separate. There was some overlap with my husband, of course, and my friend, Catherine Cronin, from our first days at Xerox, but I saw no need to expand beyond that very small circle.

The division between work and my personal life blurred with my continued ascent at Xerox. It became clearer to me that there was no way I could be successful without being more dependent on others. I didn't know a lot about business planning, for example. I didn't know a lot about law. I didn't know a lot about pensions. That required opening up to others and allowing them to get closer to me. As I continued to become more engrossed with work, the intensity around the jobs I did made it more and more difficult to have a divided life. The more I traveled, the broader my responsibilities, the more I found in common with the people I worked with. I was learning to be part of a group, a team.

Much harder to give up was my compulsion to know everything there was to know about whatever issue we were facing, especially in my mid-career. I often heard, "My goodness, Ursula, your grasp of details is amazing," but the reality was I felt I had to know because I was working with people who did know and who assumed I didn't.

Giving a speech presented a two-fold challenge. I took care to present myself in a particular way, and I felt I had to know the subject matter down to the most obscure detail. Everyone worries about how they present themselves, but I was doubly concerned about projecting an image that I belonged in that place. As a Black woman, I had to prove myself worthy of whatever position I was in because my coworkers would cut me no slack. I hadn't slept my way up the chain. I wasn't the recipient of preferential treatment. I wanted to make sure that the audience knew that I'd earned my position. To do that, I made sure they understood that I knew at least as much as anyone in the room. It was a defense mechanism against the assumption that I didn't belong.

At times, I took it to absurd extremes. I remember Anne asking me, when she was CEO and I was newly president, to give the earnings report to the shareholders. I read the earnings Q&A book two times, three times, four times, and went to the earnings prep sessions. I read and reread the accompanying document, the MDA (management, discussion, and analysis), which listed the various risks—a storm taking out the supply chain; a global economic meltdown; a legal ruling that could negatively impact our competitive position—every event that could possibly occur. I was horrified by the document's negativity. I called Anne and asked whether we shouldn't change its tone. She, in turn, was incredulous. I'd read the voluminous document that was written by lawyers for lawyers, but that's the way I was. I was new to the job and ever vigilant about not being seen as an imposter in my role.

I worked extremely hard, and that was a big positive in my career. Though it was an additional burden I carried and certainly not necessary to know it all, there could be no question about my competence. Being wildly overprepared answered the question that people had but didn't ask when they first met me: "How the hell did she get here?"

The burden eased as I became more senior and certainly when I became CEO. But even in the most senior position where I could wield power and impact, some tension remained. I felt it when addressing the company or sitting in a conference room where everyone in that space either worked for me or wanted my position. I was conscious of looking different and being surrounded by people who wished I didn't. It was a negative stereotype with an assumption of guilt. Why else did the New Canaan, Connecticut, police stop me on three different occasions while I was walking home from the train station at night? I had to live with that stereotype every day. I still do.

Stereotypes affect many people. Consider an Asian person who is not good at math. People think, "My god, what happened to you? All Asian people are good at math." They affect a blonde who is considered a bimbo, though I don't think that's the word anymore. Stereotypes create ideas about how Blacks or Asians or blondes should behave, what their competence level is, and what job is suitable for them, and it's more and more confining. It's no wonder that people were startled by the reality of a Black woman CEO, which disturbed the accepted business social order.

There was nothing I could do about being Black or a woman, and I wouldn't have changed it if I could. I liked being a novelty. It gave me a high profile among the Fortune 500 CEOs, and I used it to inspire women of all races.

I accepted as many speaking engagements as I could, especially if they were to young women. I wanted to dispel the stereotypes of the CEO as a white male and of mechanical engineers as just more white males. I wanted young women, especially minority women, to see possibilities for themselves they perhaps hadn't thought of. Yes, I was an engineer, but I was not a geek. Yes, I was the CEO of a multinational corporation, but I was also a happily married woman with children. I wanted them to see that I was a "normal" woman living an exceptional life and that they could too.

I remember one such meeting I had at the Yale School of Engineering and Applied Science. It was an open-forum discussion, and the hall was packed. Needless to say, the few young women stood out in the audience, a smattering among many young men. There were even fewer minority women. While I was there, I met privately with the women, who were members of the Yale Society of Women Engineers, the National Society of Black Engineers, the Yale League of Black Scientists, and FIRST Robotics alums. Predictably, it was a very small group.

"The good news is that you're rare, and most rare things are more valuable than common things," I told the young women. "You should be wielding a pretty big stick right about now, but you've got to believe you own that stick." I knew the women would need that confidence because of the sheer number of men in the engineering field they'd chosen and the age-old cultural bias that favors males. "A woman will say something in a meeting, and nobody will react, but then a man will say the same thing and suddenly everyone will react," I said. "I've seen this a thousand times and experienced it myself throughout my career." A lot of heads nodded in agreement. "So, speak up," I said. "Say, 'I made that point a minute ago, and just as I listen to all of you, you should listen to me.' Most of the time the guys will have no clue what you are talking about, but speaking up and educating them is better than going home and saying, 'They did it again,' or second-guessing yourself into thinking, 'Maybe I didn't say it right' or 'I did something wrong.' You didn't."

The engineering students may not have appreciated my directness. I've never had the patience to dillydally around truths that are so obvious to me. Get on with it. Black, white, women, men—they were privileged to be at Yale. They were getting a first-class education, and the doors were open to interesting careers. I hoped some were scholarship students.

The women engineers would have more opportunities than women had in the seventies when many companies resisted change. The prevailing attitude then, I often tell young women, was this: "Why bother to hire women? You guys are different, you're a pain in the rear end, you are moody, you get pregnant. I'll just keep it to the men." More and more companies realized, however, that there was a problem with hiring only men, starting with the fact that the buying public was mostly women, and slowly the doors began to open. Granted, it took gender discrimination lawsuits and imposed quotas for many reluctant companies to hire and promote women, but once we were in, we demonstrated our value. The young women entering male-dominated professions like engineering had to know that, and more important, feel their value. "If the company wanted you to conform to the norm of the man, they would have hired a man," I told them.

I used my bully pulpit at the many commencement addresses I was invited to give during my tenure as CEO, among them MIT, where my son was graduating, and Howard University, the historically Black university in Washington, DC.

I was a one-woman band on the importance and power of education and exhorted the students at MIT to have the courage to use their top-of-the-line education for change. "We're finding that some of our old assumptions and ideas don't work anymore," I told them, "and we can use people who are willing to ask, 'Why do we do it that way?' and 'How can we do it differently and better?' I almost always pointed out my inauspicious beginning on welfare on the Lower East Side of Manhattan, and I did so at Howard University. I was proud of my mother and the values I was raised with and wanted the students to know that. "Mom saw education as a way up and out of the projects," I said. "She made whatever sacrifices were necessary to see to it that I got a good education. Your parents have sacrificed too."

Amid the excitement of the graduation ceremony, I knew the Howard graduates would face challenges that the majority of MIT graduates would not. The Howard grads, for instance, would find it harder to get a job than their white counterparts. In a sobering series of studies spanning over twenty-five years, researchers tracked both white and Black job applicants with similar qualifications who interviewed for the same job. Thirty-six percent more whites than African Americans were called back for a second interview, the same racial disparity in place since 1989! I often mentioned this chronic racial impasse in interviews, pointing out the urgent need for more diversity in the market-place. "People hire people who look like them," I told *New York* magazine in 2017.

I doubt the personnel managers were practicing overt racism or sexism. They were smart enough and trained enough and socialized enough not to say out loud that this person is not getting the job because he or she doesn't quite fit our vision of that role. Instead, they were probably subject to an issue known as "unconscious bias."

What makes it interesting is if the person doing the hiring is not aware of his or her bias. The hiring agent who truly doesn't know he or she is biased, current wisdom holds, can be trained out of it. And so can employees who hold unconscious biases toward coworkers. It is worth a try. I believe that it will take a very long time, so we have to keep pushing and inspecting and measuring results.

The same does not hold true for entrenched racists and sexists. They cannot be trained out of their biases. They are the ones who are convinced that a minority is taking his or her job because of a quota system or that a woman who gets a promotion is sleeping her way to the top. They do not consider the person's merits. Their bigotry overrides everything, especially in regard to successful Black women. And so we compensate and overcompensate just for being Black and female.

Good, old-fashioned affirmative action is a potential solution to inequality in the selection of employees, allowing a greater range of people to be part of a company. We have to be willing to go into the zone of discomfort to have more rapid change. For example, one study shows that if we continue to follow the current path, it will take forty years for women, and white women at that, to achieve equal pay with men. In 2018, white women made eighty-one cents for every dollar earned by a white male, according to a compilation of studies published in *Business Insider* in 2020. The inequity increased when race was factored in. Black women earned 66 percent, and Hispanic women, 58 percent, of what white men earned. According to the American Association of University Women, white women would have to work 100 more days, Black women 226 more days, and Hispanic women 307 more days to achieve income parity with men.

The fundamental question is why. Because women deserve less? Because women are not as qualified or accomplished as men? Because women have babies? The possibilities sound more like excuses than real structural problems, especially the issue of childbearing. It's like saying men have to go to the bathroom more often than women because of some biological reason so we should pay the men less because they take more time for bathroom breaks.

There is no logical reason why a woman should make that much less than a man. The disparity was caused by a long road of bias and habit. The rules, the norms, and the definitions of what's good and how we should work are all set by white men. In many ways, they don't even know it. Corporations have failed to ensure that all of these artificial differentiators are removed when assessing performance and salary.

During my tenure, Xerox checked on pay disparity every year, and if we found it, which of course we did, we fixed it. And it wasn't just women who were paid less than white men. So were employees of color. Part of the solution was to accelerate the minorities in their jobs because, structurally, they were in lesser job categories than white men. Others we would look at and say, "There's no reason. Just fix it." Women in information technology (IT), for example, were habitually paid less than the men in IT. It took a few years to close the gap. The fact of the matter is that pay disparity should never have become a problem. We started looking at how we could stop it from happening in the first place. I still don't know the answer.

My ascendance to CEO made for unrealistic expectations. Because I was Black, female, and in charge, I was suddenly considered the agent of change for all beleaguered women or Blacks or both. Could one woman fix all the diversity problems? Impossible. Not only is the system ridiculously unbalanced but it is so aggressively structured and so historically engrained that it would take significantly more than one CEO to try and turn the ship. It would take the board, it would take the shareholders, it would take a management team that didn't need to be watched every second, it would take, it would take, it would take . . .

Much of this bias was the impetus for all I accomplished. The inequity of it all only made me more driven. I often said that being CEO also made me better: more patient, more realistic, more sensitive—attributes I had to draw on almost every day for seven years.

People, though a major expense, are the greatest asset to any company, and we had thousands and thousands of employees at Xerox. It was people who had created and run Xerox: engineers, scientists, toolmakers, salespeople, technicians, testing and quality assurance staff, and so many others. Xerox was an old-world company. A telephone caller was actually greeted by a live person. In contrast, the newer, modern companies like Google or Apple or Amazon seemed to be based on the premise that people were only added if absolutely necessary.

We started making the shift to outsourcing and automation in the early nineties. By the time I became CEO, it had become obvious that we needed fewer employees. We could use data, AI, and automation tools to our advantage and change the way the company operated by moving to more effective, more efficient, less people-intense operations. But that meant letting more employees go.

The "people" decision I was wrestling with as CEO around 2013 was whether to keep portions of our corporate finance function in the US or move it to less expensive countries around the world. The data pointed to the latter. We determined that our finance function was more expensive than in comparable industries. Yet the decision was very difficult.

The finance people were a specialized, well-educated group. They "kept the books" for Xerox, handling everything from tax strategy to accounting, revenue recognition, expense management, and more. But just as certain legal tasks or manufacturing had yielded to outsourcing or automation, so had some functions in finance. To remain competitive, we had to adjust.

I agonized over the repercussions of changing and outsourcing portions of our finance function. I recognized my responsibility to be sure, but I couldn't just throw all those people out in a changing world where they might have difficulty transferring their skill sets. Yes, we would increase profits, but would we be less human as a company? Our finance employees had invested time and energy in us and had devoted their futures to us; many had been with Xerox for twenty years and expected to remain another twenty. The decision represented a big crisis for me and the team.

In the end, we had no other choice but to eliminate some of the jobs and move the rest to Latin America or Eastern Europe. We made the transfer in the most humane way possible by giving our employees a long transition period of over a year, during which we offered them job retraining or outplacement services. We could have done the cut and transfer in less time, but we opted for the longer term to lower our business risk and to lessen the human impact of the decision.

Independent providers wouldn't even think about making the cuts immediately, but believe it or not, most CEOs will worry about the impact of the decision on their employees. They might receive unemployment insurance, but that's not enough. If they had been paid $100,000, they would receive $75,000. It might sound like you can live on $75,000, but if you were living on $100,000 just the day before it would be difficult. A CEO has to deal with a number of fundamental crises—how do you balance this and that?—and oftentimes the best answer is not perfect for anyone. It's not perfect for the employee; it's not perfect for the shareholder. Compromise is required on both sides, and most CEOs work hard to achieve a balanced outcome.

The reality is that shareholders own the company: not the CEO, not the employees, not the community at large, not the government. The shareholders bought into Xerox expecting their investment to be managed effectively. Our shareholders were from all over the world and generally were not concerned about whether we employed people in Rochester or California or Germany. Governments were more concerned about this.

Surprisingly, perhaps, I became very comfortable with this internal crisis. My firm belief was that my responsibility was not to the shareholders only, or to the customers only, or the employees or the community or the government only; it was to all of them. Often my responsibility was to select the best, most balanced choice, so we stuck with the longer transition period. It was the right thing to do.

This dilemma of home country versus foreign country, automation versus human, is a significant problem that is getting worse. Some analysts predict that at least 60 percent of the jobs of today will be gone or reconfigured over the next ten to twenty years, requiring workers to either be laid off or to learn new skills. And no one, as yet, has come up with a national policy or solution, though plenty of individuals and many different coalitions are working on it, including the Aspen Institute, MIT, and governments around the world.

America has lived through technology-driven unemployment transitions before, including the invention of the cotton gin and the introduction of robots in factories. But this transition is occurring faster than earlier ones. It is happening so quickly and so broadly that businesses and governments must act now to prepare for the future of a large number of people without useful work to do. If we don't, we're going to have revolt in the streets. I'm convinced of this.

My concern for our employees and my determination to keep as many people employed as possible was a strength as well as a weakness. It was fueled by my belief that companies and shareholders have a responsibility for more than just profit. That said, I didn't run the company like a not-for-profit. Far from it. My mantra was: "If we give you a job and you don't earn your way, you'll have to move on." But we had to let go a lot of people who did perform well and worked hard, and that always pained me.

My decisions were informed by the example of my mother, a Panamanian immigrant on welfare. She must have constantly felt close to the edge—but never showed it—as she raised my brother, my sister, and me on her own. As a single mother, she made every penny count toward our survival on the Lower East Side of Manhattan. She took in washing and ironing jobs, bartered office cleaning for our medical needs, and took care of other people's children in our apartment to supplement her welfare check. Her unrelenting concern for us and her strict demands tailored our childhoods and instilled the foundation that would govern our futures.

Her name was Olga Racquel Burns.

WHERE YOU ARE
IS NOT WHO YOU ARE

Poverty has a color—or, more accurately, an absence of color. Everything seems to be sepia when you're poor. Poverty has a persistent odor too, from the mounds of garbage the city rarely picks up, to the urine in the stairwells and elevators, to the decay in the century-old buildings. Our tenement apartment at Third Street and Avenue D in New York had all those trappings of poverty.

My mother refused to have her children be defined by it. "Where you are is not who you are," she told us time and again. I didn't know what she was talking about.

I had no idea as a kid that we were poor. Neither did my brother or sister. We had food to eat, bought by food stamps. We had a roof over our heads, however dingy, subsidized by welfare. We went to school and we had clean clothes to wear, though I don't remember ever going to a store to buy them. Perhaps the clothes were from thrift shops. My mother's clothes certainly were. Now they would be called "vintage" and be cool, but when I was growing up, vintage clothing was a necessity, not a choice. But mostly, she wore a cotton housedress.

How did my mother raise three children on little more than pocket change? Her highest annual income, I discovered after her death, was $4,400. Yet she somehow paid the fee to send us all to parochial school instead of public school so my siblings and I could get the best and safest education possible.

My sister and brother and I have talked about this a lot, how oblivious to her struggle we were as kids. In hindsight, as I said at her funeral, I can guarantee that my mother woke up panic-stricken many a morning: the food stamps hadn't come, and we were running low on food; the rent check hadn't come, and she had to plead with the slumlord not to evict us; the welfare check was late, her erratic earnings were low that month, and the school fees were due. And there we were, her kids, living merrily in our dump of an apartment without a clue. She shielded us from her day-to-day reality like any responsible parent would, but we realized as we grew older what a fundamental battle it was for her to make it through another week, another month, with no relief in sight.

Our job was to go to school, to study hard, to not get caught up in the neighborhood, to move on in life to a better place. She was fierce about it, almost maniacal. If we stepped one inch out of line, she would smack us hard. Today that would be called child abuse, but even as a child, I felt more pain from disappointing her than I did from any blow I received.

I knew very little about my mother's background until after she died and her older half-sister, Aunt Mel, told me stories about how my mother had grown up in La Boca, Panama. Even as a little girl, my mother, Olga, did not have it easy. Racism was unchecked in Panama, a bitter leftover from the slave trade, which delivered the vast majority of Africans to South and Central America, more than were exported to North America. My maternal grandmother had two kids that I know of—my aunt Genoveva, who was light-skinned, and my mother, who was dark-skinned. Racism exists in Black society too. Light-skin Blacks were considered superior to dark-skin Blacks, making Genoveva the golden girl. My grand-mother treated my mother very badly, Aunt Mel told us, so badly that she and her sister, Ursula, my namesake, took my mom away from that abusive home when she was around eight to live in their home with my mother's stepmother and father.

My siblings and I were astonished to hear all this, that our mother had been abused by our grandmother and had spent the rest of her young years living with her father's family. My mother had never mentioned it to us. Not a murmur.

I know even less about my father. What I do know is that his family and my mother's family left their impoverished villages in Panama to migrate closer to the Canal Zone, where there was more opportunity to get work. My father joined the US Armed Forces during World War II for the reward of being allowed in the US with a green card. I don't know how my parents met, but they married in Panama after his tour of duty and came to New York in the mid-fifties. I don't know why, but my mother never became a US citizen. She had a green card.

My brother, Terry, was born in 1956. I followed in 1958. Our younger sister, Deborah, was born two years later (she has a dif-ferent father), but by then my father had left us either of his own volition or because my mother threw him out. It turned out that he had a mirror family somewhere else in the city, another wife and two other children. I've never met them and have no curiosity about them nor, for that matter, about my father. I only know his name because it is the same as my brother's: Terrance Enrico Burns. I never thought I needed a father. My mother was a totally complete parent.

Think about it. Here was a single, immigrant mother in her twenties navigating a new country with no marketable skills and three children to support. She cleaned offices; she ironed; she did everything she could to make money and take care of us at the same time. When we were older and in school, she became a licensed home childcare provider and took care of other people's children. (I remember quite a few of those kids—Matthew Busby, a cute little boy with blond hair, the Lopez kids, and many others.) Somehow, she made do.

We got help from improbable sources. One was a physician, Dr. Gertstein, a most amazingly nice man whose office she cleaned on Saturdays for $10. My mother always took us with her to Dr. Gertstein's office when we were young, parking us in the reception area and forbidding us to move. He checked us out occasionally, an enormous gift: we would have had to wait in a public clinic all day to see another doctor. He also gave us medications like aspirin so my mother wouldn't have to buy them and even connected us to a dentist. We got health care outside the norm because of my mother's hard work and the kindness of strangers. Little else in our lives was outside the norm, however.

The health-care situation for the American poor has not improved much since my mom's time. The combination of free clinics, bartering for health care, the emergency room, or going without is the menu of choices for poor Americans, even for many Americans who work every day. The Affordable Care Act, known as Obamacare, was the most recent attempt to make health care more affordable for everyone. ACA has good and bad aspects, and I am not an expert on it, but the issues of lack of access due to lack of coverage or affordability remain. Many employers are offering health-care coverage of some sort to both full- and part-time employees, but, according to a 2020 Associated Press report, the number of Americans without health insurance in 2019 was estimated to be 29.6 million, or 9.2 percent of the population. These numbers are increasing in pandemic times as unemployment soars and the social fabric is fraying. The poorest Black and brown people and single-parent households are being disproportionately affected.

The tenement apartment we lived in until I was ten or so was a typical airless, very old, shotgun-style apartment with one bedroom, which I shared with Deborah. Terry slept in a little pass-through alcove, and my mother slept on the couch in the living room. We had a bathroom and a kitchen and an enduring battle with the roaches who'd lived in the building for a century. My mother was insanely organized and clean, which is one of my traits now, and kept the kitchen spotless to thwart the roaches, but even she could not get rid of the roaches. And she couldn't do anything about the building's old boiler, which periodically broke down, leaving us with no heat in the winter. The stove became our boiler. We kept the burners on and the oven on with the door open, which barely made a dent in the cold. We heated water on the stove to wash ourselves.

What she could do was to minimize anything negative. The tenement building had an elevator that rarely worked. Even when it did, we were not allowed to use it. Her fear was that it might get stuck, the lights would go out, and who knew if there might be somebody else in it? The stairs were the route to our fourth-floor apartment, but even the stairs held perils. We were not allowed to go down the stairs until my mother had gone down before us to make sure no junkies were lurking or sleeping in the stairwell.

Getting to and from school was also highly programmed. It was my brother's job to hold our hands and walk my sister and me in a straight line the three or four blocks to our Catholic grade school. To make sure my brother didn't screw up, my mother watched the daily journey from our fire escape through opera glasses she'd gotten from a thrift shop. She also had lookouts all over the neighborhood. If he deviated even the slightest bit, she smacked him upside the head when we got home.

We were very highly managed kids. When my mother went out with a friend to prowl the thrift shops on Saturdays, she made us stay in the apartment. Her rules were firm: we could not go out, and we could not cook anything while she was gone. So there we were, at six, eight, and ten, cooped up for hours and bored out of our minds. We played marathon card games and board games like Trouble, and when those got old, we played our own crazy games, like You Can't Touch the Floor. It was insane, requiring each of us to jump from the stove to a table in the hall to the bathroom and onto the couch in the living room and onward through the railroad apartment to the back of the house. We were very careful to relocate whatever was on the table so we wouldn't break anything, but my mother—who knew to the inch where everything was in the apartment—always knew what we'd been up to when she came home, and she smacked us around.

She knew, too, about another and sometimes destructive game we played by tying long strings from one thing to another all the way down the house. It was a stupid game because we couldn't undo the string without pulling, and then everything came flying down. We got smarter as we got older, but she caught us more than once. The game had pretty violent ramifications, but it wasn't as dangerous as when we would light pieces of paper at the stove, then run through the apartment and throw them out the window. We were always hungry, as all kids are, and we made crazy cornflake or Cheerios sandwiches, pressing the cereal into the bread. We cooked too, despite the ban, making eggs or frying cold cuts while one of us stood guard at the window, watching for my mother. If she appeared, we threw the food behind the stove. We weren't bad kids. Just kids.

We had more freedom, but not much more, when my mother was home and could watch us from the fire escape while we played in the street. It was not easy for her. Poverty has a pace, and the sidewalks were crowded with people rushing around in a frantic fashion, people racing great distances to save $1 here or there or hurrying to stand in line for a handout. We were not allowed off the block, and she kept close tabs on us through her opera glasses. Luckily for us there was a small park on the block with a handball court, and I got to be quite good at the game. Though we chafed under her rules, muttering to each other about her being controlling and overprotective, as a mother myself I can see the point of her rules.

The crowded streets were a gauntlet of addicts nodding off in doorways or swaying on their feet. We would look at them as we passed by on the way to school or to the little park and pity them. I have to think that the dealers had some code of conduct because they basically stayed away from the young kids. But maybe it was because there was a whole bunch of people watching in the neighborhood and keeping an eye on what was going on. They might have shooed the pushers away before they even got close to us.

Our block had a sort of informal neighborhood watch staffed by the immigrant families, most of which were led by single women. So strong were the ties among the neighborhood mothers, like Mrs. Alston and Marilyn Torres, that they could smack us—and did—if we stepped out of line. We were growing up in one of the slum "villages" of the Lower East Side.

When my brother was fourteen or so, he became the first of us who was free to roam, but not too far. My mother did everything she could to keep him busy and off the street. She gave him permission to leave the block, but only to go the short distance to the Boys Brotherhood Republic, or BBR, in the nearby community center. There was nothing similar then to keep girls off the streets. At the BBR, Terry did all sorts of stuff with his friends, including karate. He was a very good athlete in track as well and thought he was really cool—I guess he *was* really cool—and my sister and I resented him for being this hotshot, prima donna teenage boy who took too long preening in the bathroom. He often threw karate moves on my sister and me, which made my mother furious. So, like the little snitches we were, my sister and I told our mother he was doing karate on us when he wasn't, just to get him in trouble.

He was our loyal, beloved brother, however, and he saved me from various ugly situations, some involving gangs. Many gangs had moved into the neighborhood along with the drug dealers: the Black Spades, the Kings of King Shaka, the Black Magicians, and the Latin Kings, among others. They wore their gang colors on their jackets, and though they were pretty benign in the era before the Bloods and the Crips, they had knives and would mug people and just generally terrorize the neighborhood. Our mother and our "other mothers" on the block did their best to ensure that we steered clear of the gangs and weren't caught up in street fights, but one day when I was around twelve, I walked right into an ugly situation.

I was playing handball with my sister and some friends when one of the gang leaders showed up and ordered us off the court so the gang could play. Instead of complying, I gave him some lip, which was pretty stupid, and he responded by grabbing me hard around the neck and pushing me around. I was crying and stumbling away when suddenly my brother and some of his friends from BBR appeared, presumably having been alerted by one of the neighbors. My brother grabbed my hand and walked me back onto the court. "What the fuck did you do to her?" he said to the gang leader, a guy named Diego.

Diego replied, "You get the fuck out of here or I'm gonna beat your butt," and he pulled a knife.

"Terry, please. Let's get out of here," I pleaded, as the gang members started moving toward us. My brother's friends were no match for these thugs, and who could fight against a knife? I managed to get my brother away, but it wasn't over.

A week or so later, I was walking by the handball court on my way to get candy from a woman who sold it out of her window, and there, again, was Diego. "Your brother isn't here to protect you now," he said, and wouldn't you know I replied with a stupid insult, and he hit me hard. And suddenly, out of nowhere, my brother *was* there and lit into Diego, hitting him, smacking him, beating him to the ground. The other gang members held back, as did my brother's friends. It was a mano a mano fight, and my brother won. "You never put a hand on my sister again," Terry told Diego, who was blubbering on the ground. And then came the finale. My mother appeared, wild-eyed, having seen the fight through her opera glasses from the fire escape, and she let loose a sailor's trove of curses in Spanish! Everyone went slack jawed. A Black woman hurling obscenities in Spanish? At a gang leader? After that, I never had any trouble with Diego and his sidekicks.

Another time, my mother unleashed her Spanish at a dumb-founded Puerto Rican family that was insulting us. It was during the summer when the city closed off Third Street and Avenue D so the kids could play games and stickball. The city also sponsored occasional trips by bus to Bear Mountain State Park or a beach, and my brother and sister and I were going to go on one such excursion. I can't remember the destination, but I sure remember the departure. There we were in our clean clothes, holding our brown-bag lunches, when suddenly the Puerto Rican kids said, in Spanish: "Why are those niggers allowed to come on the trip with us?" My mother overheard them and told them off with words they understood.

That confrontation was not physical, but there is no doubt that there was a lot of violence in our neighborhood, particularly in our parochial school. The nuns and the lay teachers were overwhelmingly strict, even cruel. They beat us for anything, smacking us on the hands, legs, and rears with ten rulers held together with rubber bands. And we couldn't go home and complain because our mothers would beat us up as well. If the teacher beat you, then you must have done something wrong, they reasoned. The brutality was horrifying.

The sensibility of today regarding physical punishment did

not exist in the sixties and seventies, at least not in my family, neighborhood, or school. Adults had complete authority. Interestingly enough, I did not, and do not in hindsight, believe it was all that bad.

I got my share of whacks in school, but not half as many as my sister and brother. I was more compliant. I figured it was my job to go to school and study and not throw a tantrum, like my sister did, about having to wear a uniform. She wanted to wear shorts, not a skirt, so she could play basketball, so she wore shorts under her skirt. Deborah was much more in-your-face than I was, but I had my moments too.

One such moment occurred on my very first day at the school. My full name is Ursula Maxine Burns, and my family called me Max or Maxine at home to avoid confusion with my aunt Ursula. To the nuns, however, I was Ursula, even though I kept asking them to please call me Maxine. Whack. And I'd ask again. Whack. My mother finally had to come to the school to calm things down and convince me that Ursula was my given name and the name I would be called at school. I was okay with it after that.

I was not okay on another occasion, when I said something that the nun found offensive and she slapped me. I lost it and yelled at her. Whack. Whack. Whack. And she expelled me for the day. The school called my mother to come pick me up, and that caused a crisis of its own because she had all these kids she was taking care of and she had to bundle them up because there was no way in the world that she would let me walk the three blocks home alone. She was very angry, having had to make that same trip several times before for my brother and my sister. "Your job is to teach them, not beat them up," she said over and over to the teacher, then proceeded to really take it out on me when we got home.

I was the only one of my siblings to make it all the way through the eighth grade. My sister was expelled for fighting back—and my brother for resisting a really vicious beating in the fourth grade. Each exit was a reaction to the nuns' intractability, and to be honest, I admire my siblings.

It's really interesting talking to them now about our time in that school and how differently we saw it. My brother and sister see it in terms of racial discrimination. The nuns and lay teachers were all white, they point out. So were most of the students, many of whom were Jewish. My brother remembers there were only eight or so Blacks in the entire school. My sister remembers there were only three in her class, plus a few Latinos. I didn't really notice or care. I just wanted to get through the damn place.

My brother is still bitter about the inequity of his treatment. At the beginning of his fourth-grade year, for example, he was caught talking in the line during the class lavatory run, and for the rest of the term, he was made to sit alone in his own row in the classroom. In contrast, white kids who were caught smoking in the bathroom or cursing got off lightly. "Why was talking in line so bad?" he says. "Only thing: I was Black."

His persecution grew to involve the entire family. One of his violations resulted in his having to copy every word in the dictionary from "a" to "b." We were used to punitive lists of our own, having to write "I shall not _____" fifty times, but copying every "a" word in the dictionary required the whole family to sit around the kitchen table scribbling so he wouldn't be beaten, though I'm not sure we cared much by the time we were through.

But Terry continued to be beaten at school. The final act began, as Terry tells it, when the lady in the school cafeteria insisted that he have ice cream for dessert, but Terry said no, thank you; it was strawberry ice cream, and he was allergic to strawberries. She persisted and Terry said no, he couldn't and would just throw it out. She pressed it on him, and he threw it out. The nuns were waiting for him with the rulers when he got upstairs and said he'd been disrespectful. They smacked him on his knuckles, on his back, on his shoulders, on his behind, and he resisted them, trying to protect himself from the blows. That did it. My mother was called to take him home, and she faced down the nuns. "Did you ask him what was actually going on?" she said. I don't know what their response was, but the end was near. Two weeks later, my mother was back at the school again. The issue this time was the chocolate bars the students were supposed to sell for $15 to benefit the school; somehow, he'd lost the chocolates. The nuns insisted my mother owed them the money, which she didn't have. Pay up or he will be expelled, they threatened. She took him out of the school that day and sent him to public school where, in his words, he "blossomed."

That whole chocolate bar incident was so unfair and unrealistic. Who, please tell me, were we going to sell the chocolate bars to? We could sell maybe three, but my mother was supposed to come up with the money for the rest. That was a huge problem for her, with three children in the school, but the nuns didn't care. There were rules . . .

My sister's expulsion was easier to understand. She fought and fought and fought, and the nuns beat her and led her around by her ear and made her stand in the corner on one leg, but Deborah was tough. "A hard head makes a soft behind" became one of her favorite sayings. Just a few weeks before she was due to graduate from eighth grade, she was thrown out of the school for bloodying a bully's nose on the basketball court, and she joined Terry in public school.

My mother was very religious, but in a nontraditional way. She didn't go to church but held novenas in the apartment and invited her women friends in to light candles and say special prayers. One of her prized possessions was a big, heavy, ivory (or faux ivory) rosary that my Aunt Mel had brought her from Italy. The rosary hung on the wall along with a picture of John F. Kennedy and an optical illusion piece of Venetian glass—if you looked at it straight on, you saw Jesus Christ, and from the sides, it was the Virgin Mary or God. I was going to bury the rosary with her when she died, but my aunt said absolutely not, and I'm happy I didn't. Deborah, who is quite religious, has the family artifact now in her apartment in Rochester.

I wasn't very religious, but I went to church six days a week! We had Mass every single morning before school; we had Saturday off but had to go to church again on Sunday and twice a day during the holy seasons of Christmas and Easter. My brother was an altar boy, and I did whatever you had to do in the formal church system: confession, first communion, confirmation. The whole Mass was said in Latin then, with the priest standing with his back to the congregation, and though I didn't understand a word of it, I apparently memorized it. Years later, when I was visiting Aunt Mel in Hawaii, we went to church and I found I could recite most of the Mass along with the priest.

I started going to confession in the first grade. We had to. I didn't have much to confess at the age of six, so I made up some stuff: I lied to my mother four times; I had bad thoughts about the nun; I cheated on my test. And the priest would say, "Okay, for those sins you should do four Hail Marys and three Our Fathers." I would then leave the confession box and kneel down among my schoolmates and do my penance. The process was very transparent. Everybody knew if someone had sinned a lot because that kid would be kneeling for a long time reciting multiple Hail Marys and Our Fathers.

Though confession at such a young age may seem ridiculous, it was in fact quite formative. Every week leading up to confession, you had to think about what was right and what was wrong. I often thought, "I don't want to have to do twenty Hail Marys, so I'd better not do that." There was something useful about the penance when I was young. I told the priest everything I could think of because I thought he may have known anyway. Fear was a great behavior modifier.

I outgrew the mystique, of course. I became cynical as I got older and manipulated what I was going to confess, then stopped going to confession altogether, followed by avoiding church itself. I haven't been back. The Catholic Church is not in tune with my ideals anymore. In addition to the revelations of the sexual abuse of so many children, the church's structure hasn't evolved with the times. If it continues to operate the way it has for two thousand years, it will continue losing people. Like many others, I've joined a huge and informal congregation of "lapsed Catholics." There is hope, however, with the current pope. Francis, who is known as the "reform pope," has reached out in a meaningful way to the divorced, the LGBT community, the world's desperate refugees, and the poor. He often puts on a priest's plain habit and goes to visit homeless shelters at night. He even had one built right next to the Vatican.

I think my mother was right in pursuing her own expression of religious belief by holding novenas with her friends. We thought at the time she was crazy, of course, and we were furious at her for not letting us go play outside when she couldn't watch us, but if she got any sense of peace, it was worth it.

My mother did not have a whole lot of time for relaxation, but she loved bargain hunting for treasures in the thrift shops. One day she brought home an old record player on which my sister played the Jackson Five over and over and my mother listened to Charley Pride; she had a crush on the superstar country singer. She brought home plates, all different sizes and shapes, which made them a nightmare to put away after we washed and dried them. Another time she brought home a felt-lined wooden box with various old silver spoons, knives, and forks in it. We ate with those for years.

Not everything she brought home had a function. She also had an artistic side and collected glass objects—blue glass, green glass, clear glass—no matter whether they were vases or ashtrays or animals. We found so many in her apartment after she died that they filled thirty boxes. My husband and I moved those boxes to Rochester, where we were both working for Xerox, then to New York City, where we had different assignments, and from there back to Rochester. I couldn't bear to let go of that last connection with my mother until finally, after thirty years of lugging the boxes around, my sister and I, helped by my husband, went through the boxes, selected a few pieces for ourselves, and put the rest in a dumpster.

My mother hoarded canned food, too, which was more understandable. My aunt Lillian, my mother's sister-in-law, said the hoarding habit came from my mother's early days in the Canal

Zone during World War II, when there was the constant threat of attack. During the many air raid drills, my aunt's family lowered dark shades, turned out every light, and huddled together in one room. The uncertainty evidently had a great impact on my mother, and she addressed it by using her food stamps to buy and store every sort of canned food. Everything we ate came from a can—peas and carrots, beets, corn, those horrible Vienna sausages. I didn't see brussels sprouts or fresh broccoli until I was eighteen, nor did I have undiluted orange juice. My mother always added four cups of water instead of two to those frozen Tropicana tubes so the juice would last longer.

Despite the limitations, she was an outstanding cook and quite famous for it. She would whip up something for anyone who stopped by the apartment—pork and beans, eggs and cheese, and our favorite, *bakes*. She must have brought the recipe with her from Panama. *Bakes*, a staple in the Caribbean, is a sort of fried bread made out of flour, sugar, yeast, salt, and baking powder, all ingredients she bought with food stamps. We got to put a little butter on the *bakes*, and it was delicious. She also made a really good oxtail stew and *baccala*, another island dish, with the salt cod she always had in a box in the back of the fridge. Restaurants now present *baccala* as an artisanal dish, which always makes me laugh. We grew up on that stuff because it was cheap. She often served the salt cod with onions and canned tomatoes.

Aunt Lillian was an even better cook. She lived in Brooklyn, and my mother used to visit her as often as she could on weekends, especially in the summer. They knew each other from Panama and were good buddies. Often, my mother wouldn't get home until one in the morning, having had to take the train, which was a long walk away. When we got older, she'd sometimes take us with her to Brooklyn as well as to Jamaica, Queens, to visit another aunt, Ursula. (We called it Long Island, but it was Queens.) Ursula, known as Cita, was one of the sisters who had rescued my mother in Panama. The other, Mel, was married to a member of the Air Force and lived in Greece. My aunts and their families had a lot more money than we did. My uncle in Queens, Cita's husband, owned a tailor shop, and every year he and my aunt gave us Christmas presents and new Easter outfits. They had a bigger television set than we did; it had rabbit ears and striped vellum over the screen to simulate color. The effect wasn't perfect, but it sure looked better than ours. And their furniture! I will never forget going to Queens one day and seeing all the brand-new furniture in my aunt and uncle's house. We never had a piece of new furniture, and here was a whole living room's worth, covered in plastic. (She never took the covers off, and the plastic continues to protect the now fifty-year-old furniture.)

By economic standards, my relatives in Queens were middle-class, albeit barely. They owned their own house with a little patch of lawn, and most treasured, they had a car. They were generous, and like all close families, we took care of each other, as more relatives were arriving from Panama. My mother's sister Genoveva, the light-skinned one, moved in with us for a while. So did my cousin Napoleon. (He was the son of Napoleon I, whose brother was Napoleon II, both sons of—guess who?—Napoleon!) Our Napoleon, known as Fellow, was a wonderful friend to all of us. My cousin Lily, whom my aunt Mel and uncle Robbie had adopted while Robbie was stationed in Greece, lived with us for long periods of time over the years. That she and others stayed with us, the poorest members of the family and with the least room, reflects the love everyone had for my mother. Even on her worst day, you knew she would feed you, you'd have a place to sleep, and you'd be safe. And you could sit on the furniture.

Our family, like most Black families, does not identify members as "half" or "step" or "adopted" or whatever. We basically have brothers and sisters and aunts and uncles and cousins—a custom Deborah learned the hard way as a kid. Deborah, whose last name is Eastman, called me her half-sister one day because I am a Burns, and my mother whacked her hard. "I am the mother and the father," she told Deborah. "I wear the pants and the dresses in this family. And that's your sister!" Deborah, who is now the most amazing woman, never made that mistake again.

My mother was very clear about a lot of things. Calling someone "stupid" was one of them. "Not a good word," she'd say. "'Ignorant,' maybe, of the facts and circumstances, but 'stupid' is a mental defect, and if you jump to that conclusion, then it takes all the burden off of you to try and understand the context of what the person is trying to say." She was just as absolute about right and wrong, and she did not accept any excuses for doing something wrong. Being "nasty" to anyone fell into the "wrong" category, regardless of any excuse we might come up with to justify being less than charitable.

She practiced what she preached. She believed strongly that we were all responsible for each other. And though we were really poor, she acted on her belief by helping people poorer than we were with food, clothes, and other items she got from thrift shops. She often cooked for and fed others. I don't want to give the impression that she was a saint. She had a sharp tongue and a mouth that would make a sailor blush, but she had a firm set of morals and strong personality traits, many of which I inherited.

She was very impatient, as I am. She was always moving, multitasking, fixing things. She didn't have a lot of people to count on, so she did everything herself. A stopped-up toilet? A bad grade? If there's a problem, let's try and fix it. And we didn't dare to complain about anything. Whining and pouting were red flags to her—and to me. For years at Xerox, I had a sign in my office with WHINE in capital letters with a line through it.

My mother also had a compulsion for order, which she passed on to me. I make lists of everything, label storage boxes, and tidy my desk every day. Over the years, I stored copies of everyone's passports, including those of my brother and his family, collected medical records for my sister, though she hadn't asked me to, and planned every detail of every family vacation. I felt comfortable being on top of every conceivable situation until my daughter asked me to back off. "This may be helping you," she said, "but it isn't helping me."

I also inherited my mother's lack of need for a male partner. She never gave me the impression that she needed a man in her life to do anything. In retrospect, it would have been easier for my mother to have had someone to at least help out financially, but she didn't seem to care, and nor did I. I never felt I was missing out on something that an "intact family" would have offered my siblings and me. Our early lives as a family had revolved around my mother, and hers around us. How lucky we were.

We had more room when my mother's application for admission to the Baruch housing project finally came to the top. God knows how long it took for the application to get through the process, but it moved us a rung up the ladder. It was a huge step for us to leave our tenement, where we were at the whim of a landlord, and relocate to the massive public housing project run by the city. There was such promise at first—a superintendent who lived in the building, elevators that worked, little play areas outside—but over time we faced the same issues: the elevator was always broken, there were no lights in the stairwells, and the familiar smell of urine pervaded the building. In today's parlance, it was a freakin' disaster but slightly less disastrous than the tenement.

The actual move was a nightmare. We didn't have a car, and we couldn't afford a moving company. We had help from some friends. We walked back and forth with shopping carts filled with boxes. We carried our couch, our kitchen table, our four chairs. We didn't have a lot of stuff, but it felt like a ton that day. People on the street chipped in for a minute or five, especially when we moved the beds, but we didn't have the money to pay them, and that was all right. The accepted practice was that someone does a favor for you, and you do a favor for them. There was a fundamental respect for certain people in the neighborhood, and my mother was very well respected. She was calm, she wasn't mixed up in neighborhood dramas, she didn't gossip or loiter. Young people from the neighborhood helped us, and so did my brother's friends and my friends and Napoleon, who showed up at some point with his broken-down car. And that's how, when I was ten, we moved into Baruch Houses. My mother lived in the projects for the rest of her life.

Baruch was a city unto itself. The public housing development was huge—seventeen buildings, thirteen or fourteen stories tall, spread over twenty-eight acres! There were some twenty-one hundred apartments housing over five thousand moderate- and low-income people.

Our first apartment had two bedrooms, which was an improvement over the tenement. My mother knew the drill and immediately put in her application for a larger apartment. We were on that list for two years or so before we moved to a three-bedroom apartment in another building, this one at 60 Baruch Drive. We were still short a bedroom and only had one bathroom for the four of us, but we made do. Somehow, I got my own bedroom, as did my brother. My mother and my sister shared the third bedroom. Inexplicably, there was a freezer in one of the bedrooms, and my mother started hoarding frozen chickens. Whenever she got a little extra money, she bought another chicken.

The apartment had an infestation of roaches, even though my mother kept it fastidiously clean. She came up with a deadly roach cocktail involving borax and sugar. She put the mixture on the kitchen floor, and the roaches ate it and died, but then another generation arrived. She fought them and fought them, and we probably had the smallest population in the building, but we could never get rid of them entirely.

Our third-floor apartment was Spartan but adequate. Walking out the door, however, was fraught with danger. My mother resumed her habit of walking down the stairs before she let us come down. The stairwells were dark, and junkies lived permanently under the stairs, peeing, defecating, and shooting up in what they considered their "house." Taking the elevator was again out of the question. Not only was it almost always broken, but it had more potential dangers than the one in the tenement. The neighborhood watch we'd had in the tenement had its equivalent in a building watch at Baruch. Parents watched out for all the building kids trying to get safely home to their apartments without being mugged or beaten up.

Outside the building, there were mounds of garbage everywhere. And rats. It wasn't the residents' fault. Hundreds of families lived in the buildings, but the city only sent in a garbage truck once every ten days! My mother was disgusted that there was no official effort to keep the place fundamentally clean. The inevitable chain reaction was set in motion: People in the neighborhood expected it to be dirty, and the sanitation workers expected it to be dirty. The officials threw up their hands at the ongoing filth, and no one in the neighborhood was motivated to even try and keep it clean. I was fairly oblivious of all this as a kid, but I realized as I grew up that this was just one example of the institutional neglect of poor people. The poor were often put down—and they still are. People in more affluent neighborhoods expressed amazement at our living conditions and asked how we could live like that. Well, we had no choice.

I realized also that the police were part of the conspiracy of neglect in their indifference to the gangs and drugs. You could walk up and down the streets of our neighborhood and see dealers selling drugs openly and gang members fighting and the police doing absolutely nothing. If I had been a police officer, I would have had the greatest arrest record on the force because people didn't even have to hide. Why bother? As long as the drugs and the gang violence were contained in our neighborhood and didn't spill over into another, the police looked the other way. The common excuse was that if you arrested one drug dealer, another would immediately take his place, so what was the point?

We were kept in our place, both literally and figuratively, trapped in a triangle on two sides by water—the East River and New York Harbor—and on the other side by the vast developments of Stuyvesant Town and the upscale Peter Cooper Village. There was a fence with locked gates around Peter Cooper. We could look in to see a land of green grass and clean, neat, tree-lined paths and fountains, but we couldn't go in. All-white Stuytown, as it was called, with Peter Cooper in the northernmost part of it, had its own private police patrol armed with batons and pepper spray just to make sure we didn't intrude. Created after World War II for returning veterans, the Stuytown developments did not accept Black tenants.

What Stuytown and another nearby twenty-one-story development, Masaryk Towers, did have was window guards. Following several instances of children falling out the windows of high-rise buildings in the seventies, the City of New York required the installation of window guards on every apartment with children under ten. Peter Cooper quickly installed them. All the fancy buildings around us installed them. The Baruch Housing Projects did not. I don't know if Baruch has window guards even now, though I expect they do because there is so much transparency today. At the time, however, it was just another example of the inequality in society, an unevenness we would get glimpses of through the fence surrounding the lushness of Peter Cooper Village and our non-childproof windows. Most people in our neighborhood didn't spend a lot of time worrying about those things, however. They were just trying to figure out a way to make it through the day.

BECOMING ONE FLESH

I was on my own journey at Baruch, propelled by having my own room. My mom always stressed that I had to find my own place, not physically but emotionally. My sister and brother did most of their living outside, doing sports, hanging out with friends. I didn't. Instead of going outside, I stayed home and read. I think it was my way of avoiding the world. Among my favorite books was a series of love stories written by Andrew Greeley, a Roman Catholic priest. I read a lot of history books too, not scholarly books about the American Revolution, but books about people in history, like John Adams and Alexander Hamilton. I was an avid reader, and I consumed the books I took out from the nearby public library or that were given to me as presents.

My sister and brother both had outgoing personalities. I was kind of introverted. I thought I liked spending time by myself, but in retrospect I'm not sure I actually liked it as much as I got used to it, and then it became what I liked. I don't know if there was a reason I chose to spend so much time alone, but I practiced it so much that I became very good at it. I still am. I have a few close friends, but most of the time I prefer to be alone. I am fine in company meetings, but if I have the choice of going home or to a party, I'm going home. I am not into small talk and find that the conversations generally end up being about the same things. Maybe it is a pattern I learned as a child, but my nature, or maybe my training, actively pulls me away from superficial social engagement.

Most of my living is between my two ears, and always has been. Even as a kid, I was able to disengage from all the noise around me and process whatever feelings I had or information I needed and quietly come to a conclusion. My brother and sister were different. They would argue with each other and even with my mother, with predictable consequences. Talking back to her started a chain reaction. If she said, "No, you cannot go downstairs to play" and the chorus was "Why?" she'd say, "You're fucking with my patience." If they persisted, she would totally lose it and whack them. I rarely talked back to her. That does not mean I didn't have likes and dislikes and anger and resentments, but I kept them to myself. My mother knew when my silence was not quietness and took it as an insult. "God doesn't like ugly, Maxine," she would tell me time and again, somehow knowing that I was having mean, deceitful thoughts. "God doesn't like ugly." What an amazingly impactful, scary statement. I say it now to my kids all the time.

There was never a question whether I would go to a parochial high school. I was on that track from the first grade on. The only question was—which one? I took the Parochial High School test in eighth grade and did well enough to get into my first choice—

Cathedral High School. My choice had to do with geography. Cathedral was on the east side of Manhattan and would be easy for me to get to by taking the nearby First Avenue uptown bus.

I was supposed to be in the inaugural class of Cathedral's new building at 350 East 56th Street, but it wasn't ready for the start of the school year. Instead, my classmates and I had to go to high school in a temporary building in a really bad neighborhood on 42nd Street and Eighth Avenue. Now, of course, the area has been completely gentrified. In 1972, however, it was a den of sex clubs, rundown hotels, and sex workers.

So unlikely was the setting for young girls to be going to a Catholic school that the New York Archdiocese arranged for the police to meet us at the Eighth Avenue subway station and escort us to the building. The whole thing was a nightmare, including the giant pain for me to get there and back from the Lower East Side. I had to take three different subways, never knowing if they'd be running on time—or at all. Every day was a nail-biter, and the ordeal went on for months until we could finally go to the new building.

I got my first glimpses of a different world through the bus windows on the ride to Cathedral High School, from East Fifth Street to 56th Street. We only had bodegas and pizza shops in my neighborhood, and services like hair styling were provided out of people's apartments. In contrast, I began to see hair salons and little clothing boutiques for women and restaurants with international-sounding names that didn't look like they sold pizza. I also saw people walking dogs wearing little coats. I thought this new world was pretty cool.

My brother had discovered this world from the seat of his bicycle. Every weekend he and his friends rode their bikes through all the boroughs—the Bronx, Queens, Brooklyn, Staten Island, and Manhattan. They rode through Central Park and Prospect Park and up Fifth Avenue and down Park Avenue, so he was far more worldly than me. My boundary was 56th Street. I rarely went above it until I went to graduate school, and then I only went uptown to the West Side and back by subway. It would be years before I spent any time above 56th Street on the East Side.

Cathedral was a different world as well. My grade school had fed from the neighborhood, but Cathedral drew from all five boroughs of New York, a very broad reach. There were a lot more white girls than there were nonwhite. But more important, Cathedral had a broader set of kids both socially and economically. There were poor kids like me, poor kids who were a little less poor than me, middle-class kids, and even upper-class kids. You could tell by who got picked up by a car after school and who went on vacations. I had never even heard of a vacation before.

Despite these differences, there were similarities that bound us. We were all girls. We were all Catholic. And we all wore school uniforms. There were cliques, of course, certainly among the girls who were driven back and forth to school and the athletic girls. But the tone of the students wasn't exclusionary. I interacted with all of them, and though I wasn't one of the most popular girls, I wasn't unpopular either. I was a pretty middle-of-the-road kid and uninterested in the various extracurricular activities, like the yearbook and sports. I didn't have a desire to belong to anything, though I would have been welcome to join, which made it easier because I didn't feel left out.

What I was interested in—and learned at Cathedral—was sorting out my priorities. I became very aware of the things in my life that were worth fighting for or getting engaged in. One issue that some girls were pressing for—the right to wear makeup to school—was definitely not one. I had an aversion to changing the way you look to appeal to other people. Perhaps it came from my mother, who didn't wear makeup, but my attitude hardened in high school. With me, what you saw was what you got, including, at that time, a huge Afro.

I found my voice at Cathedral in challenging what I perceived as illogical rules. It wasn't an in-your-face challenge, but a more acceptable way for me to obey. In the past, obeying to me meant just shutting up and going along with the rule because the fight just wasn't worth it. In high school, I learned to argue and debate and to make a point, and I discovered that sometimes reasonable challenges actually caused things to change.

A case in point was the dress code at Cathedral. In the beginning, wearing the school uniform was very comforting to me, as it made us all the same. As time wore on, the rules became ridiculous, though. We had to wear skirts and white short-sleeved shirts that buttoned up with a little bow tie that crossed in the front and snapped into place. We couldn't wear pantyhose or stockings, but we could wear tights and socks. Every inch of our bodies was regulated.

It was the socks that got to me. They had to be blue, and I tested the rule by sometimes wearing checkered socks with blue in them or blue socks with a green stripe or a red stripe. Time and again I was told I had to take the socks off because that was not the uniform and could never wear them again or I'd be written up for the violation. I'd argue politely with the nun or the lay teacher that the rule was silly, and then I'd be sent to the principal and I'd articulate the same message and still get in trouble. If the nuns found my argument rude, I'd be given detention. That meant a variety of things: extra homework, double duty as a hall or stair monitor, the loss of a break period and reassignment to the library—all sorts of things. I got my share of detentions and established a reputation among the girls as a rebel.

I wasn't, of course. We were teenagers and just trying to differentiate ourselves. Some girls wore symbolic pins supporting various movements like women's equality on their bow ties and were written up for that. Others took license, as I did, with the blue sock rule and suffered the same consequences. Eventually, we got together as a group and went to the principal, made our argument that the rule was silly, and got it changed. It was a useful rebellion and a lesson I took away from high school.

My all-girl school made it easy for me to feel comfortable around women. Though I was rarely in that situation as an adult, the older I got, the more I realized that societal norms cast women as a deficit, and though I do not dismiss men who also work hard and have a strong work ethic, they don't have to deal with the constant "What are you doing here?" We didn't have to cope with that bias in high school because it just wasn't there. We discovered our own strengths and bonds as women and could draw on that reservoir pretty much forever. My single-sex school was perfect for me. I really needed it.

I didn't hang out much with the girls outside high school but that was for no reason except that it wasn't convenient or manageable. It's hard to remember, but back then, we had no cell phones and no way to communicate with our families except by pay phone. Unless plans had been set in advance, there was no option after school except to hightail it to the bus and go home. Your family couldn't contact you to find out where you were if you broke a predictable pattern, so the rules were pretty clear in my family and in all my friends' families: no dallying after school.

I didn't mind the routine: Go home. Do your homework. Do whatever chores you have. Then have time for yourself. I remember that free time being a big deal for me—getting through all the requirements of the day so I could do what I wanted. I'm in my early sixties now, and it's still a goal for me to get through my required tasks and then sit down and have the ability to do absolutely nothing.

We had school outings, of course, for which permission slips were required, signed by the parent. We went to the usual places— like the Museum of Natural History, the Brooklyn Botanical Gardens, the United Nations—and then went directly home. The school discouraged any hanging around at the building, primarily because of the uptown neighborhood the school was in. The school didn't want any complaints about noise from its tony neighbors. We were instructed over and over not to raise our voices.

There was, however, a lot of noise and unrest in America in the seventies. Women were marching and striking for equal rights, equal pay, and equal educational opportunities. Students and liberals were protesting the Vietnam War and managed to force a new law lowering the voting age from twenty-one to eighteen. The Black civil rights movement was fighting to implement the changes made in Lyndon Johnson's civil rights legislation, which passed in the sixties, though the initial promise of equalizing public schools by busing white and Black kids out of their neighborhoods was backfiring and causing white flight to the suburbs. As a result, the inequity in the city's public schools just got worse.

The Vietnam War didn't really affect me personally, but it did our neighborhood. We saw the guys leaving and the guys coming back with PTSD or drug addiction. We didn't hang out with them, but we saw them from afar. More relevant to me, though I didn't know it at the time, was the women's movement. I was barely a teenager and not involved in the movement, but I was becoming more aware of how much society devalued women. Women in the mid-1970s made only 59 cents for every dollar earned by men for similar work, for example. Graduate schools offered only a small percentage of available admissions slots to women applicants, and women couldn't even have a credit card in their own names. I'm not sure I even knew what one was, but I was puzzled by the lack of respect for women. The women I knew, especially my mother, were stronger than many of the men I knew.

Much of the civil rights movement had taken place when I was younger. I was only ten when Martin Luther King was murdered, and I remember watching the coverage on our little TV when we were still living in the tenement. I wasn't much older when the Black Panthers came to the forefront, and I was very impressed. They were organized, articulate, well-dressed, and confident and were willing to stand for something that had to do with us Black people. The Black Panthers and others drummed the reality of race and poverty into the public consciousness—and eventually into mine. It wasn't until I started taking the bus uptown to high school that I recognized the inequity they were talking about.

I embraced the movement when I was in high school. I wasn't a militant, nothing near that level, but I got involved. I marched.

I went to rallies. For the first time, I recognized the reality and meaning of the blatant racial imbalance in this country, which tipped people like me to the bottom. Funnily enough, I heard the terms "Latino" and "Hispanic" for the first time in high school. I'd always thought of all Spanish-speaking people as Puerto Ricans. Whatever they were called, they were at the bottom with us.

We were living through the Nixon era, a really hateful time toward people of color, especially Black males. The president's so-called war on drugs, launched in 1971, turned out to be not only about drugs but a means to target and incarcerate Black men and anti–Vietnam War activists. It was purely political. Neither group had supported Nixon in his 1968 campaign, so he used the law to demonize Black men as heroin dealers and users and to lock them up, eventually increasing their incarceration rate fivefold. "We could arrest their leaders, raid their homes, break up their meetings, and vilify them night after night on the evening news," John Ehrlichman, Nixon's domestic policy adviser told Dan Baum, author of *Smoke and Mirrors: The War on Drugs and the Politics of Failure*. "Did we know we were lying about the drugs? Of course, we did."

Even I was shocked reading about Nixon's bold and punitive racism in *Harper's* magazine in 2016, realizing that it all played out when I was a naive teenager in the seventies. I embraced the Black pride movement, which was the most positive. The focus was for Black people to celebrate themselves and respect their facial features, hair, and dark skin color instead of trying to look "white" by straightening their hair and even bleaching their skin. "Black is beautiful," the rallying cry of the new consciousness, was huge in my life. The message was exclusive. It meant that if you were white, you were *not* beautiful, a complete reversal of accepted biases. I put a "Black is beautiful" sticker on my bedroom wall and started to let my hair grow. My Afro grew and grew during high school.

I was a really good student. I got awards for all sorts of things in the tenth, eleventh, and twelfth grades. I excelled at math and science and writing—not creative writing, but sentence structure, grammar, penmanship, taking notes, doing outlines, and the like. I wasn't the number one girl in the school. I wasn't the valedictorian or the salutatorian, but I wasn't into that kind of competition. The competition I was in was against myself, which is the best kind of competition.

My mother was pleased but not surprised by my awards at Cathedral. She had very high expectations for her children, a fact that had been very clear to me every step of the way from first grade on. Her attitude was simple: "I am not giving you a reward for doing well at high school when there is no other thing in the world you could possibly be doing right now. You are doing what you are supposed to do."

It was financially insane for my mother to send me to Cathedral. I can't imagine the sacrifices she must have made. The tuition was $55 a month; that's $650 out of the $4,400 she earned in her best year. She was sometimes late on the payments, and the school administration either gave me a note to bring home to her or asked me to ask her to come in and talk to them. There was never a threat, to my knowledge. The school was forgiving and reasonable. I am sure they admired her for her determination and sacrifice to give me the best education possible.

At least I didn't have to ask her for money. I made my own by working every weekend, after school, and every school holiday. The most accessible job was as a cashier at Woolworth's on 34th Street, right across from Macy's. The hours were flexible and you could get there by public transportation. The pay wasn't that great, and the work was kind of boring. Still, it was reassuring to know that if nothing else worked out, you'd always be able to get a part-time job.

Summer jobs were more of a challenge. The city and the Police Athletic League mobilized all kinds of projects to keep high school inner-city kids off the streets—and working. Everyone wanted one of those jobs, which generally paid quite a bit more than the minimum wage and weren't grunt work. You had to start in March researching what summer jobs would be available and then apply, apply, apply. Cathedral helped a lot with the process, but it was very competitive. There were maybe fifty jobs and five hundred applicants, but if you didn't get one of those interesting and fun jobs, you could always fall back on being a cashier. I was really lucky and got one of the plum jobs for two summers in a row— pulling weeds in Central Park. The job was offered through the Henry Street Settlement, a venerable social service agency on the Lower East Side where my cousin Napoleon worked as a dance instructor and counselor and gave me the inside track for the job.

I loved those ninth- and tenth-grade summers. Central Park was in serious trouble in the early seventies. The infrastructure was falling apart, the crime rate was high, and the trees and shrubs were being smothered by *Persicaria perfoliata*, a wildly destructive strangler vine known as "mile-a-minute." The counselor for our project was a guy who was studying horticulture, and he taught us a lot about the weeds, the importance of having a variety of plants on hills, and the tons of rats we were displacing by disrupting their nests and resting places. It was a really cool job, and it paid well that first summer and even better the second summer because I came in at a higher level. I later joined the Central Park Conservancy, mostly because of those two summers, which marked the beginning of the very successful movement to rejuvenate the park.

There were so many programs back then for poor people, people of color, and women. The nation's consciousness was being raised by the organized pushback against structural inequality. The goal of many programs was to equalize opportunity and quality of life for all Americans. I am saddened—outraged, actually—at the current and increasing disregard for the poor.

It was as a teenager at Cathedral that I began to recognize the unrelenting pressure on my mother, both financial and personal. For the first time, I realized that she had devoted her entire adult life to her children, giving us everything she had to maximize our possibilities. I had never thought of her before as a person with her own needs, but selfishly through a child's eyes as someone who was there to feed us, clothe us, look after us, and essentially work for us. She didn't do a whole lot for herself. She didn't date. She didn't drink, save for the tiny little bottles she had of Miller beer on occasion. She was always tired, and I began to understand why. Everything was always a little bit heavier for her. Would the welfare check be on time? Would the food stamps be enough to feed us as we grew? What extra work could she get to pay my tuition? She lived on the edge of survival with no buffer between her and financial collapse.

The realization hit me hard, and I was determined to help her out. I found a possible solution by accident. In tenth grade I had taken the practice college-admission test known as the PSAT—everybody in the city took it—and I had done very well in math. I don't know whether Sister Rosemary, Cathedral's guidance counselor at the time, even looked at my math scores, however, before advising me. "You have three choices, Ursula," she told me. "You can be a teacher, a nurse, or a nun."

That was discouraging, but luckily, and I really mean luckily, I met with a more worldly part-time college counselor who came occasionally to the school. "You've done really, really well in math, Ursula," she said to me after reviewing my test results. "You should concentrate on advanced math courses for the next two years to be competitive for college." The problem was that Cathedral didn't offer many, which prompted my later campaign for STEM classes to be offered in every school possible. Cathedral wasn't well-funded and did not emphasize math and science. Still, it was a phenomenal school for someone of my background, though marginal for families with means. (I support the school to this day. It continues to excel in the basics and has become an outstanding school for math and science as well. I am so proud to be an alumna.)

My strength, I'd learned, was math, but how could math translate to money? I found the answer in the public library pouring over *Barron's Profiles of American Colleges*. Along with the descriptions of the colleges, I chanced on a page on career choices that showed the highest-salaried occupations for first year graduating students. Number one: Chemical Engineer.

Done. Decision made.

The process of filling out application after application for different colleges was daunting. "A whole lot of people apply to these schools, but only a few get in," I remember telling my mother. And I remember her response: "We actually have no concern about 'a lot of people.' We only have to worry about you. So stop telling me all these hypothetical things, and get down to it and do the best you can." The tuition costs for college were also staggering. Even with the Tuition Assistance Program (TAP), the gap between the money provided and the actual tuition was more than twice my mother's annual income. I had no idea how we were going to make it happen, but it was clear it had to happen. Going to college was not a choice.

DON'T LET THE WORLD HAPPEN TO YOU— YOU HAPPEN TO THE WORLD

Affirmative action admission policies had taken hold in many universities and colleges following the revelation of gender and race inequities spurred on by the women's movement and the civil rights movement in the sixties. It's really important to understand the significance of that. If people hadn't taken a look at how things were done at that time and decided to make a change, I, and many others like me, would never have been able to go to college.

I applied to many colleges but not to those whose requirements I thought were ridiculous. One of the schools that I really wanted to go to required students to swim a lap in the pool to graduate. You might think the requirement was designed to ensure water safety for all students, but I am convinced that it was a really clever way to discourage inner-city kids. How is an inner-city kid going to get to a pool to learn how to swim?

I have no doubt that the swimming requirement was just one of the many screens put in place to try to limit a certain type of student. The SAT was another. The standard college-admission test was skewed toward the knowledge and language that white suburban kids would have. There was a question involving the word "regatta," for example. Another, if I remember correctly, concerned the word "camber," which is the upward curvature of a ski or something similar. Very few inner-city kids would be familiar with yacht racing or skiing. Whether the bias was conscious or unconscious, the outcome was a lower acceptance rate for underprivileged applicants.

The College Board briefly tried a new Adversity Score for the SAT, which took into account a student's "disadvantage level" based on multiple factors, including the neighborhood crime rate, the poverty level, and housing and class size. The good news was the recognition that standardized tests often fail to measure applicants' full potential. The bad news was that, while this new score attempted to capture an applicant's unequal opportunity, it also hid the need for a total reexamination of standardized testing as the basis for college admissions.

Our high school graduation was held in St. Patrick's Cathedral on Fifth Avenue in Midtown Manhattan. We all wore white robes and mortarboards and were very careful not to get them dirty because they were rented and we had to return them. It was a great celebration. My mother came. My brother and sister came. A whole bunch of aunts and uncles and cousins came.

It was all the more festive because I'd gotten into quite a few of the colleges I'd applied to—Yale, Carnegie Mellon, Columbia, City College, Brooklyn Polytechnic, and maybe some others that I don't recollect. I chose Brooklyn Polytech (now New York University) because of its location: it was only four stops away on the subway. I could take the F train to the Jay Street / Borough Hall station, or if I had to, I could go by foot over the Brooklyn Bridge. I was accepted through the Higher Education Opportunity Program (HEOP), created by New York State in 1967 to aid economically and educationally disadvantaged residents. Polytech told me my situation, financial and educational, made me eligible.

The program was essential. HEOP paid my full tuition and gave me a stipend for the subway and food. If I'd taken out loans through the Tuition Assistance Program, I would have been in debt for $80,000. My entire goal was to make money to help out my mother, but I would have left school with more debt than I could have paid off before her death.

HEOP provided support as well as money. The program began during the summer after I graduated from high school and included around twenty-five of us from all over New York State— Black, Hispanic, white, immigrants. Our common denominator was poverty. We were counseled about the books and equipment we would need, about the classes we should choose, about the extra help we might require. The program soothed my nerves about taking such a huge step from the neighborhood. My mother also gave me courage. "Don't let the world happen to you," she told me in a much-repeated instruction. "You happen to the world."

And so it was that in September 1976, I got up, put on the clothes I'd ironed the night before, kissed my mother goodbye, and left the Baruch housing project to catch the F train to my first day at college.

Chemical engineering. What was I thinking? I had taken only

two chemistry classes in school and was in way over my head at Polytech. I might have dropped out of college at that point, as do so many overwhelmed, disadvantaged students, but to my great fortune, the HEOP counseling continued after the school year began. After talking to my counselors, I switched to mechanical engineering, which presented challenges of its own. I realized right away how poorly prepared I was in advanced math. A lot of my new classmates had been to tech high schools like Bronx Science, Brooklyn Tech, and Stuyvesant. They had a huge head start in that they were at home with slide rules, calculators, integral calculus, labs, and so on. I had some knowledge of such things, but I was far behind them. I found great study partners—a mix of fellow HEOP students and others—and we helped each other. HEOP's expectation, which proved to be correct, was that with some effort and focus, students like me would catch up. Though I entered college with a big gap between me and the much better prepared students, all of them white males if I remember correctly, I caught up quickly. At the end of the first semester, I was tutoring other HEOP students.

Like many others, including my brother, who went to Syracuse University through HEOP, I got a start toward a productive future because some taxpayers paid a little more money for programs like HEOP. I think of them as patrons acting out of the goodness of their hearts. Under the Trump administration, which tried to eliminate race as a factor in access to higher education, we were institutionalizing bad hearts, and that is tragic for all those who need just one break to cement a better future.

My brother and I were lucky. Our sister, Deborah, was not. While my brother was doing well at Syracuse and I was holding my own at Polytech, Deborah dropped out of high school in the tenth grade. She had always been rebellious, the only one of us to push back against my mother's control and expectations. Deborah had always thought of herself as different—she was gay, for starters, and had a different last name. She was also incredibly spoiled by my mother. In any event, she got mixed up with a bad group of friends in the East Village. It took decades and caused a lot of family heartache before she finally straightened out. She has long since become my greatest inspiration and has the warmest heart in the family. I admire and respect her tremendously, as does my brother. Deborah and I are very close and speak almost every day. I really, really like her.

What I didn't like was the racism, or at least the racial stereotyping, which I encountered head-on for the first time in college. Almost every student in my classes was a white male, and my presence seemed to astonish them. "You're still here!" they said when I returned for my sophomore year. I was an oddity to them: odd in my ability to complete a sentence, odd in my ability to do integral calculus, odd in my ability to communicate well. "You're so smart and articulate," they often told me in an amazed tone. "My goodness, you really are good at calculus." How did they think I'd gotten into the school? I had taken the same admissions tests they had. I got there because I was good at calculus. "Why do you do so well in math?" I was asked. "Because I study hard," I said.

It always came back to students of privilege asking the questions. I didn't fit their perception of what a person at that college should look and act like. It wasn't that they were mean to me (they weren't); they just couldn't comprehend how a Black girl could be as smart as or, in some cases, smarter than they were. So, they made a special category for me. Unique. Amazing. Spectacular. That way they could accept me.

The college fed into it too. I was just one among the twenty-five or so students with a 3.2 or better average who got into Pi Tau Sigma, the international honor society for mechanical engineers, yet I was the one who was continually called on to speak, to be on the cover of the mechanical engineering magazine. The other students treated me like royalty, which I interpreted as a way to rationalize my presence in those robes. They had to categorize me as exceptional, a pattern that continues to this day. If they didn't, they would have had to come to the realization that any Black person could make it there, and this is something they certainly did not want to do. But I didn't let it get to me. I had more immediate concerns.

My small stipend from HEOP for food and transportation, which I supplemented with weekend and holiday work at Woolworth's and side jobs like babysitting, wasn't enough. There were days when I had only $2, but I made it work with a slice of pizza and maybe a Pepsi for lunch or a falafel off a cart for 70 cents that filled me up and left enough money for the subway home. My fellow HEOP classmates, the people I hung out with, also had to stretch their money. Today my kids don't even think about money. They just go to the ATM. But for me, making do on a bare minimum was a life experience that would serve me well in later years at Xerox.

I started interning the summer after my freshman year. HEOP hosted corporations on campus, and I was recruited for two summers by Western Electric Engineering Research Center in Princeton Junction, New Jersey. The first summer I commuted from New York by train, and the second summer I lived in a Princeton dormitory with other interns and went home on weekends, often hitching a ride to the train station on the back of a motorcycle belonging to a young up-and-coming engineer at the company.

How fortunate I was to have HEOP and the experience of summer interning. I wish all kids, especially poor kids, had access to internships. Mine was life-changing, for sure. I had to separate from home and live in a different city, a huge step for me. I had been out of NYC only once before for a brief visit with my aunt in Florida. The whole idea of working and having to get work clothing was entirely foreign to me, as was mixing with the engineers at Western Electric who were much older than me. And I was one of the few female interns and one of the very few people of color. My world suddenly became much larger.

One of my managers was named Roland. He was a seasoned engineer who did a lot of his work on a slide rule, which was interesting because we were into handheld calculators by then. It was helpful that he was Black, a person I could more easily identify with. It was encouraging to me that Roland had a very good position in the Fortune 100 company, that he was very good and very competent. His presence definitely made the work environment more comforting and familiar to me.

I worked under Roland's tutelage. My mission was to measure minute temperature variations using thermocoupling devices that were thinner than a hair; any movement would cause them to break. It was very tedious, but it was interesting and pretty cool too. To get one measurement often required fifty attempts because the thermocouple broke constantly. It was a lesson in patience and precision. I enjoyed the work, putting into practice what I'd been studying at school.

I also enjoyed getting a weekly salary for the first time, as my former jobs paid by the hour. The salary I was making as an intern was fairly good and went a long way toward bankrolling my next year in college. But the internship was much more than money. It showed me a completely different world from my day-to-day life on the Lower East Side of Manhattan—people who worked in a big company, people who drove cars to work, people who earned a significant amount of money. For the first time I realized that could be me.

I thought I'd try something new at the end of my junior year and accepted an internship at Xerox. I had two more years before I would look for a permanent job, and an internship was a great way to look at a company and for the company to look at me. Xerox was very different from Western Electric. The people there were more engaging and curious about who I was, and they wanted me to come back to work for them. At Western Electric, the internship was more about evaluating potential employees than about introducing them to the company. At Xerox, the interns spent a week in orientation in Leesburg, Virginia, where we were told the history of the company and xerography, the technology that made Xerox, Xerox. It was a different approach, and I liked it.

Another reason I chose Xerox—I'd also been offered an internship at General Dynamics Electric Boat (the submarine company) in Groton, Connecticut—was that Xerox was in New York State, which meant to me that it was close to home. It wasn't. Xerox's manufacturing headquarters turned out to be way upstate in Rochester, about as far away from home as I could get and still be in New York. But I was lucky. Freddie Laker had started Laker Airways by then, and the round-trip fare to New York was only $39 and sometimes as low as $19, so I flew home on lots of weekends. I was living in a dorm at Rochester University and didn't have a whole bunch of stuff to do around town, so I flew to New York to see my mother and my HEOP friends from college who were doing their own summer internships or had jobs. Like me, they were poor, and their summer salaries were critical in helping them get through another year of college.

My intern work at Xerox was interesting and varied. I did some lab work as an assistant to various scientists, among them Barry Wolf, a Columbia University professor who ran MESA, Xerox's Mechanical Engineering Sciences Area lab. I also analyzed data from experiments, did some business case analysis, and learned a lot about Xerox on sponsored outings. It was a fun and informative internship.

All my hard work almost came to naught during my senior year, when I came close to dying from a ruptured ovarian abscess. My fever skyrocketed to 104 while I was home for Christmas break, and the doctor sent me in an ambulance to the emergency room at Metropolitan Hospital. The burst abscess had poisoned my body, which led to IVs of antibiotics in my neck, in my arm, and through my nose to my heart. I was put on a cooling bed to lower my temperature. The doctors finally operated and removed an ovary and a fallopian tube. I was in the hospital for ten days and missed some class time, but I recovered. In the spring, I graduated cum laude and was recruited again by Xerox, this time for a permanent job.

I wanted to go straight to work but was counseled by Howard Adams, who ran an organization called the National Consortium of Graduate Education for Minority Engineers (GEM), to get a master's degree. At the time, a lot of international engineering students with advanced degrees were coming to the United States, looking for jobs. Howard convinced me to stay in school and get at least one other set of credentials after my name to be more competitive, especially as a minority woman. Xerox was eager to sponsor me through GEM, and I reluctantly agreed to another year of education. I just wanted to hurry through all the hoops and start making money for my mother.

I was fortunate in that I was single and still living at home when I went to grad school. Nowadays, more students seem to be in relationships or have their own families, which makes graduate school much harder financially. Nonetheless, I continue to urge every young person going into engineering to try to get at least a master's. At this point, an undergraduate BS degree is close to having just a high school diploma. "If you're rushing into the job market because you think you're going to lose out if you don't," I tell them, "don't do it because it's really rushing out into a world where more and more of your competitors are going to have better credentials, particularly people who are not from the United States." Some people can go to work and get a master's at the same time, and I support that if somebody's willing to pay and their families can get by on less. Others going into the pure sciences like biology, chemistry, and physics may actually be better off going straight to work, where they can learn the same if not more on the job. But if they're doing mechanical engineering, I advise them to continue at school if they can afford to.

I'm a huge champion of engineering as a career. It's a great field to go into, with a broad set of opportunities. Today's world needs a lot of the solutions only engineers can develop. We produce lots of waste; where does that go? We want greener buildings; how do we build them? How do we make airplanes larger or fly faster? Conversely, how do we make electronics smaller and cheaper? Every single goal is literally a set of problems that engineers work on and nobody else can solve. Engineering is a growth business for sure, and we need more Americans to pursue it and join their highly educated colleagues from India and China.

I worked for Xerox during the summer before grad school and met my future husband, an accomplished Xerox research scientist. Lloyd, who was divorced, had extra rooms in his house, which Xerox rented for interns. I was one of them. The three others were African Americans from Georgia. I had not spent much time around southern Blacks before, and my presumption was they'd be farmers and hicks, but instead they were well-spoken, very well-educated, and funny. We had a great time with one another and with Lloyd, a renowned cook whose weekend barbeques were legendary. He used to drive us to work in his big old car in the mornings.

That fall I went to Columbia as a GEM fellow. Xerox paid me a salary of $110 a day as a consultant for a certain number of days while I earned my graduate degree in mechanical engineering. Grad school turned out to be a very good move. I got a lot more experience by doing independent research, working in a team, and solving problems. I graduated with honors, to the amazement of many of the white students who couldn't understand how a Black girl could do so well. I had to be an exception. I had to be amazing.

My mother was still living in the projects, but I was definitely trending toward the middle class, as was my brother. Terry had graduated from Syracuse and was training in high-altitude running in New Mexico in the hope of making the US Olympic track team. A terrible car accident ended that dream, and he went to law school instead. He ended up working in Internal Affairs for the California Department of Corrections and teaching legal issues to law enforcement communities.

My mother was very proud of my brother and of me while working hard to keep my sister in check when, armed with my master's in mechanical engineering, I started working full-time for Xerox in 1981. I stayed for thirty-six years.

ZIG AND ZAG

We are standing safely outside the lab, watching the thin glass disk inside spinning faster and faster. Our engineering task is to redesign the raster output scanner (ROS) to make it really quick at scanning and more affordable. We hold our breaths. Will the disk hold? Is there any unevenness or wobble? Is it cool enough? The revolutions per minute mount until we pass 1,000—and the friggin' glass blows apart. Again. Back to the drawing board. We finally succeed by using an O-ring mounting system and a thin rod with a core in it that makes sure the glass vibrates as little as possible. It takes us two years to figure out the solution, but it's satisfying.

I struggled at first to understand how to fit into this white corporate world. I wore skirts and a little jacket to work, like all the other women, but I didn't feel comfortable. *This isn't working*, I said to myself after six months, and I switched to wearing pants. I felt much better.

It was amazing to me how different this world was from my own, including the music. I worked in a Xerox office in Webster, New York, when I first started and listened to the music of Rick James, Al Green, and Marvin Gaye while I drove back and forth with my car window down. A car with a white driver drew up next to me at a traffic light one day, and the music she was listening to was entirely different, country-western or something. It happened the next day and the next. I was dating Lloyd and remarked on it. "The conventional wisdom is that calling attention to yourself is not a great thing when you're different," he said, "so here are a few solutions. Either turn your radio off, turn it to their station, or keep it just where it is and keep going." I kept it tuned to the music I liked. It seems like a minor choice now, but it had a huge amount of symbolism for me at the time.

Over the years, I passed on Lloyd's advice to other minority women in the company—Black, Hispanic, whatever. They had gone to great schools and were exceptionally talented, so they didn't need job counseling. My mentoring was more about being comfortable in their skin. "The system is not designed with you in mind. It's designed with other people in mind," I told them. "It's not easy to describe exactly what 'that' is, but you can feel it for sure, and you are going to have to maneuver it without losing who you are and without losing the technical and individual capabilities we hired you for."

As for me, I did every job I was asked to do at Xerox, zigzagging from one engineering project to another. I knew there was a career path leading to, say, chief engineer, but I was not particularly concerned about that path in the beginning and definitely did not want to do this job to be a grade 6, then that job to be a grade 7. I thought of Xerox as a family business, and like any family member, I was willing to do anything to help it succeed. If someone said to me, "We need an engineer, Ursula. Can you do this?" I inevitably replied, "Sure, I'll try it." I wasn't being asked to sell drugs or beat the inmates. They needed an engineer.

My experience and philosophy stand in stark contrast to the millennials, who have contracts and when offered a job ask, "How much am I going to get paid? What is the title exactly? What's the benefit for me?" These are important questions, and it's correct to ask. But I didn't get into any of this positioning until really late in my career. I literally didn't care, didn't know, didn't think about it. I just loved working. I loved the idea of going to an office and trying to solve complex problems and feeling the sense of accomplishment when I did. I was really into analytical work, problem solving, planning—that type of work. I didn't have a lot of other things to do. I wasn't married, I didn't have children, and I was totally engaged in the company. The job was fun, the projects were challenging, and the work paid well. I was not focused on a career path, but on the task at hand. I didn't get involved with office politics or my progression. I just put my head down and did whatever I was asked to do. I zigged and zagged, which stood me in good stead. I met a lot of people and earned a reputation as someone you could count on for help.

Xerox turned out to be a wonderful company and perfect for me, though I didn't know that at first. I had little to compare it to, but I liked what I saw. The culture was blue collar with very little hierarchy. People at the highest level carried their own bags, drove their own cars, ate often in the company cafeteria, and mostly flew Coach. The company culture was very people oriented. Problem solving involved discussion, debate, and consensus all the way down to my entry-level work in various engineering labs.

Many of the employees had been there for years and years. There was a sense of family and loyalty at Xerox, which had a far lower rate of turnover than other companies. The pay and the benefits were good, vacations generous, and health coverage excellent. There was also a first-rate tuition reimbursement program. The company had a strong social conscience as well. The Xerox Foundation supported all sorts of programs in the communities from which Xerox drew its workers, contributing to schools and universities, the arts, environmental groups, and social services.

The company also supported and encouraged in-house affinity groups for women and minorities, including the Women's Alliance and the National Black Employees Association. I joined both groups but found them lacking. The Black men weren't paying enough attention to the Black women's issues, and the white women had their own issues and weren't paying much attention to the Black women. Because we could fit in either group, we were forgotten in both, so we started our own group, the Black Women's Leadership Council (BWLC). There were very few of us—I could literally go a month without seeing another Black woman employee—so getting together was really important in terms of confidence building, relaxation, and information.

Thirteen of us met for the first time in 1986 to form the BWLC. We had no idea where Black women stood in the company or if anyone even knew we were there. We started to mobilize and asked many questions. HR supplied us with the data we requested on promotions. "How come none of these people are Black women?" we asked ourselves. "Is there something we're missing?"

Our meetings were as much consciousness-raising sessions as anything else. For example, female employees, both Black and white, had kept silent for years about their discomfort with the "girlie" posters and calendars some men kept on their desks, particularly in manufacturing. For the first time, we talked to each other about it and agreed not only that it was inappropriate and disgusting but that it represented women's lower status in the company. It was all part of the sexist package. That simple realization, along with our interactions at the BWLC, was a growth experience, for sure. We became more confident, both individually and as a group. We definitely became more polished in setting forth our opinions and arguments, and we learned how to listen more and better. To have a meaningful impact, we had to forge a partnership between the BWLC and HR and become a positive part of Xerox. Our role was to make Xerox better, and our mechanism was to ensure that Black women progressed in the company. In the process, we grew up and found our voices. Mine was perhaps too strong at times, but it was mine.

To its great credit, Xerox embraced all these groups. We had speakers, some of whom were senior leaders from inside the company, some from outside. In time, the company gave us what they called senior level "champions," intentionally mixing the races and genders. The Black women would have a white male champion, for example; the Hispanics, a Black or white woman; the gay group, a straight person. Basically, the philosophy behind the program was that nobody can think outside the box if everyone comes from the same box. The goal was to expand the horizons of the senior champions about the very different experiences each group had, enabling them to become better employers.

Working with these different groups was an eye-opener for the corporate champions. Our champion at the BWLC was Mike Mc-Donald, a white guy who was head of sales in the US and probably had the largest single cadre of Black women in the company. Some of our salespeople were very tenured, but a lot came straight out of college, so it was very useful to have Mike as a champion. He recognized that diversity was a high priority at Xerox and did a great job. Another champion who did a great job was a straight Belgian woman, Sophie Vanderbruck, PhD, who ran our research function and was made the champion of the gay, lesbian, and transgender group. Sophie became such a good champion that when she rotated out after two or three years, she was one of the strongest and most progressive voices in the company in the area of diversity around sexual orientation.

I was active with the BWLC for years, sometimes serving as its vice president. No matter how senior I became at Xerox, I never stopped being a Black woman. And though many companies now have similar groups, Xerox was among the first, if not the first, to showcase diversity, which is not surprising considering the company's history.

The Xerox Corporation had been a pioneer in diversity since it was founded in 1906 by Joseph Wilson, a Rochester native. During the social upheaval of the sixties, race riots ignited in Rochester, prompting Wilson to take an enlightened position. He began hiring minority and female employees. "Why is it that we have none of these people working here?" he reportedly said. "I cannot run a company that is called a great company where the Blacks and women I see out my window every day are literally not here."

My husband was a beneficiary of this new policy. Lloyd was a brilliant scientist but could not get a job in the government because he was a green card holder, nor in the private sector because he was far from conventional. Joe Wilson hired him, and Lloyd went on to patent more inventions for Xerox than practically any other scientist in the company at the time.

Wilson's philosophy continued after his death in 1971 with the new CEO, C. Peter McColough. He persuaded his friend, Vernon Jordan, to join the board of directors at Xerox in 1974, well before Black members were really considered for board positions elsewhere. McColough took diversity aims very seriously for Xerox based on the long-term statistical projection that white men would steadily dwindle in numbers and therefore it was in the company's best interest to have trained women and minorities in place to offset the loss. Recruiting women made particular sense, especially before women entered the workplace in great numbers. While Xerox might recruit among the top 10 percent of men, the theory went, the company could go after the top 1 or 2 percent of women because few other companies were interested.

I was only twenty-four when I bought a house in Rochester, where the houses were actually affordable. I was making $29,000 a year, and the house cost $55,000. It was a great house, and I was so pleased when my mother made the huge trip to come visit me. I was concerned, however, when she slept a good deal of the time. I blamed plain tiredness. In addition to being a licensed childcare provider, my mother had joined an incentive program funded by the city for low-income women and was going to La Guardia Community College in Queens once a week to get an associate's degree. She really liked it, but it didn't last.

About a month after her visit, my cousin Napoleon (Fellow) called to say that my mother was in Bellevue Hospital. Bellevue was a horrible place then, providing care to only the very poor and the insane. My mother was in intensive care and delirious when I got there the next day, babbling about her mother and her sisters back in the Panama of her childhood. The doctor said she had hepatitis C. Her liver was failing. She improved enough to be moved into a room where she was hooked up to all sorts of machines, but the doctor called me that night to say she had died. She was forty-nine.

I have beaten myself up about her death ever since. I am convinced that with better care she wouldn't have died. I was only twenty-five. I didn't question the doctor or the decisions made on her behalf in the hospital. I visited her, and then I left. I didn't manage her care as I would today. Now I would insist on learning every detail about the disease, demand to know the latest research, and get her to the city's top expert. Years later, when my husband was having serious surgery, I grilled the doctor and instructed the nurses to turn off the beepers and the lights in his room and not keep going in to check his vital signs when they could read them on a monitor at the nurses' station. He needed his sleep to recover, and he did. But when my mother was so sick in the hospital, I was inexperienced and accepted the authority of the white-coated doctors.

I'm haunted by the many what-ifs. What if she hadn't been so poor, if she'd been able to afford a private doctor, if she'd gone to him or her sooner? Maybe she could have been treated for hepatitis C early on instead of entering the hospital in critical condition. (I'd sent her money, but she obviously hadn't spent it on her health.)

What if she hadn't still been caring for other people's children? She didn't catch hepatitis C from eating oysters or drinking or taking drugs; it's likely, I learned later, that she got it from the feces of a child whose diaper she was changing.

In hindsight, I realize some of the things I should have done. I should have been a better advocate for my mother. I should have understood that having money and a voice or, as in our case, not having money and not having a voice, can fundamentally change the quality of care you get. To the hospital administration, my mother was just another poor person on welfare. Her care was paid for by the state and provided in a sprawling hospital that was underfunded and stressed because of the neighborhood it was in. She was no one special. She was one of the many, many dots on the board in Bellevue, a hospital that was trying its best to provide health care to people who couldn't afford the best, who didn't have great advocates, who didn't get care early enough. Like so many others today, my mother was a victim of poverty.

I remember very little from that awful time in 1983. My aunts and cousin helped out a lot with the funeral, and several of the families whose children my mother had taken care of over the years came to the service. I was told she needed clothing to be buried in, and I went to May's department store (the poor person's Macy's) and bought her a big, flowy housedress. I think that was the first new dress she'd owned during her entire time in America, maybe ever.

My mother's death turned my world upside down. It changed absolutely everything, and in retrospect, some of that change was good. I became pretty solid around the set of morals she'd drummed into us and adopted certain of her personality traits, like her obsession with order and her impatience with laziness and wasted time. Still, I felt lost without her.

I found solace in my close friend Catherine Cronin, who had been my roommate at the Xerox new-hire orientation course. She was my lifeline and introduced me to the very progressive Corpus Christi Church in Rochester, whose leading-edge priest, Father Jim, would shortly be removed from Corpus Christi for allowing women to participate in the church service, for marrying gays, and for housing poor people and refugees. I was a lapsed Catholic, but I responded to the true Christian spirit of his church by helping to paint walls in local schools, build houses, and serve lunch at the men's homeless shelter, a charity supported by Xerox. I followed Father Jim to his new, underground church, Spiritus Christi, whose services were held in bowling alleys or movie theaters, but I had to give it up when I started traveling extensively for Xerox.

Xerox began dispatching me on engineering jobs to England, to California, to Japan. It might be normal now, but back then, sending a little Black girl all over the place to work, to create a new business model or a new something else, was a big deal.

Xerox had a long-standing partnership with Fuji Film in Japan. Fuji Xerox made small machines for the Asia-Pacific markets, while Xerox US made large machines for our markets. The challenge I and the other members of the Xerox team (a business planner and a marketing guy) inherited around 1988 was to work with Fuji Xerox on our first joint venture development project, the Century 5100, which printed a revolutionary one hundred pages a minute. As a technical specialist program manager (TSPM), I traveled back and forth to Japan every few months for five long years.

My role was to manage all the details and schedules—the design elements, the performance reviews, the delivery of parts like the windshields and the wheels, the integration of it all—and to report upward to US management. A particular challenge was working with our Japanese counterparts: they spoke some English, way more than we could speak Japanese, but not enough to understand nuances. I became pretty good at reading body language and understanding the unspoken stuff we had to be sensitive to.

I loved the physical beauty of the countryside of Japan. I loved the food, and I had good relationships with many individuals. Still, Japan was my least favorite destination at the time. I was 100 percent foreign in Japan, and it was hard to avoid feeling like an "alien," the terminology used for non-Japanese in the airport where the immigration lines were divided into "Japanese" and "Aliens." I often felt like I was from Mars. Everything about me was different. I was tall. I was a businesswoman, which was very unusual in Japan at that time. And I was Black. People would stop and stare at me—literally—when I walked down the street. Kids would stop and point.

Our Japanese business colleagues were a bit more worldly and at least did not gasp out loud when I entered the room. But when I went outside, I'd hear the sharp intake of breath from everyone I encountered. The people just went into shock when they saw me. It got old very quickly, especially for a girl who'd grown up on the Lower East Side of Manhattan, where we might not have had a lot of Japanese businessmen running around, but there was significant diversity.

To be fair, this occurred over thirty years ago. The average Japanese person then had not seen a lot of Black people. It was also well before the internet and international television. Even computers were brand-new. The Japanese lived in a very uniform society, particularly outside Tokyo. When I went to the Fuji Xerox location in the Japanese countryside, I was probably the first Black person the people there had ever seen. It took me quite a while to realize that their reaction to me wasn't their fault. They were not trying to make me feel uncomfortable. It was nothing personal at all. I was a pioneer at that time, though an unwilling one.

Thinking of Japan brings back a host of other nightmares, mainly about getting there. I hated the ten-hour trip, particularly after I had children. There were no cell phones then, and I felt so panicky being out of touch that I used to cry when I got onboard the plane. One phrase kept running through my brain in an endless loop: *This is not where I want to be*. I had more than enough air miles to upgrade to Business Class, and I'd eat the little portion of caviar and sour cream they'd give us on United and then drink one mimosa after another. The drinks would knock me out for three or four hours, but then I'd wake up and still have six hours to go.

I felt even more remote when we landed and got to the hotel. It cost a fortune to call home, and because of the time difference, there was no good time to call—or be called. As a result, I stayed in a high state of anxiety the whole time I was in Japan, and it didn't help to have strangers gawking at me.

Even working with Fuji Xerox from Rochester was a challenge for all of us. Scheduling phone calls at a reasonable time was almost impossible because of the fourteen-hour time difference. The language difference also made communication difficult, as did communicating by fax. Japanese copy paper was shorter than ours, and any fax from us to them was cut off at the bottom. It was more productive to deal face-to-face with Fuji Xerox personnel, so back I went to Japan, time after time, mimosa after mimosa.

Fuji Xerox was a very important joint venture for the company. Xerox was facing stiff competition from IBM, Kodak, Minolta, Canon, and Ricoh, along with many Japanese photocopying companies. Fuji Xerox's advanced technology for making small and light low-end machines for export to Asia and Xerox's European markets (and, eventually, the US) helped Xerox beat back the competition. So important was Fuji Xerox that hundreds of Xerox employees were dispatched to live and work in Japan, while a lesser but still considerable number of Japanese workers were sent to Rochester. Among them was Chu Yamamoto, who became CEO of Fuji Xerox while I went on to become CEO of Xerox. We grew up together in the engineering functions of the two companies and became friends.

I was so relieved when my regular travel to Japan came to an end in 1991 with the launch of the 5100 Century copier. I went back many other times but not with the frequency of those early years. I loved being home, doing interesting new jobs at Xerox, and seeing Lloyd, who had become more than a friend and adviser. I was a business planning analyst for a new computer printing module for a year or so, then a module engineer for a bigger, mid-volume machine, then back into business and product planning, working for Tom Adams, who was the head of that division.

Tom was a very interesting man who made a strong impression on me. He was Black, an Ivy League graduate, and an impeccable dresser, but he could have been white. Everything about him was the model of a stereotypical white businessman—the way he dressed, his beautiful wife, Roz, his daughter, the car he drove, the way he spoke. Tom showed me a whole new example of what success looked like.

Tom, my third model of Black achievement, was very different from the others. The first was my husband, Lloyd, who was smarter than you can imagine in an area that most people don't understand. His brain carried him totally. He had a big Afro and a beard, and he was not a typical businessman at all. He was so good at what he did, which was so specialized, that in order to get the value he brought, they had to accept him. My second example of success was Vernon Jordan. When he walked into a room, the dynamic changed, and everyone looked at him. When he opened his mouth, the room silenced and listened to him. He was a strong, powerful, bigger-than-life Black guy. Tom was not, which made him such a good example. The men I had been dealing with were super-humans to my mind. I didn't work for Tom that long, but for reasons that are not totally clear to me, he always stuck in my mind.

MENTORS AND MODELS

I attended an internal meeting in 1989 called by Xerox management on the Quality of Work Life. Lloyd had urged me to go, if for no reason other than to get me out of the lab, where he thought I was spending too much time, and to participate in the rest of the company. I went to the meeting out of curiosity, wondering if it was going to be a kumbaya type of thing, when a young, white male asked the convener, "Why do we hire women and minorities? Doesn't that lower the hiring standards of Xerox?" I listened with increasing anger as the guy chairing the meeting said no, the company was not lowering its standards. I raised my hand. "I'm surprised you gave his question any credence!" I said angrily. "Why not attack his assertion directly?" At the end of the meeting, the chair stopped me. "Please see me in my office," he said.

I vented my disagreement and dissatisfaction to Lloyd when the meeting ended. "Do you know who called that meeting?" he asked. "That was Wayland Hicks, the number two person in the company." Wayland was the executive vice president in charge of running Xerox's marketing operations worldwide, he told me.

I was convinced I was going to be fired when I walked into Wayland's very odd office. There were no chairs and no ordinary desk. Wayland had a bad back, it turned out, and there was only a tall desk behind which Wayland stood. I braced myself, anticipating bad news, but instead, he chided me for my reaction to the young man: not for the substance of my objection, but for my blunt and inappropriate presentation. And thus began my long personal and professional relationship with Wayland.

Wayland invited me to come chat with him once a month about what was going on in engineering and to share whatever was on my mind. We had many discussions about Japan and the challenges of competing with Japan as a company and as a country. Japan was not well liked then in America. The belief was that the Japanese companies were gaining ground, partly through excellent work, partly through unfair means. We spoke often about how to compete better, how to be more efficient, and how to attract, train, and retain more women and minorities. Wayland believed that America's diversity was a secret weapon.

Our discussions and frequent arguments were far ranging, including cultural personalities like Bobby Knight, the controversial basketball coach of the championship Indiana Hoosiers. Wayland admired him, but I didn't; I considered him to be kind of a tyrant. Back and forth we went in our many debates about countless subjects. Though I didn't know it, I had become part of Wayland's mission to identify and mentor young engineers with potential, particularly women, and to make sure they had opportunities to move around the company and grow. I was about twenty-eight, and from then on, I was on his radar.

Too much on his radar, I thought when Wayland asked me to be his executive assistant. "Why would I want to do that?" I asked him, thinking it would be just a glorified secretarial job. Besides, the EA position entailed moving from Rochester to Xerox's executive headquarters in Stamford, Connecticut, and Lloyd and I had just gotten married. It was Lloyd who told me I would be a fool if I didn't take the job and the career opportunities that could come my way, so I packed up and moved to Connecticut without him. Xerox had a shuttle then for employees who flew back and forth between Connecticut and Rochester, and I either caught the flight or made the five-hour drive. Lloyd came down by train on occasion, but there was no point in him moving to Connecticut because, increasingly, I was rarely there.

I traveled the world with Wayland: to London, Tokyo, Toronto, Mexico City, Paris, Dusseldorf, Madrid, everywhere. At five in the morning, we'd jog together and talk before a day of meetings and hours and hours of sitting. We talked nonstop as well on the many car trips we took together to Xerox facilities, including an unplanned one when the invasion of Iraq caused our plane to be diverted from White Plains, New York, to another airport near Hartford, Connecticut. We argued the whole way home in our rented car—Wayland supporting the hawkish Bush administration, me suspicious of it. We enjoyed the easy relationship of colleagues who spent a lot of time together and had respect and affection for each other.

I learned a lot about leadership by watching Wayland operate. He was very hard-driving and had an intensity about work—you don't stop until the job is done—which was quite exhausting. Because he worked nonstop, so did I, delivering papers to him all hours of the day or night, constantly moving around the country and the world. He was a puritanical, principled leader and, believing that we all got paid quite a lot, refused to abuse the company's money. There was nothing more important to him than earning every single cent that he made, and we ate at McDonald's and flew Coach on our marathon trips to Europe and Asia.

Wayland, who remains a dear friend, gave me specific leadership advice. He urged me to hone my bluntness by advising me not to intimidate people and to listen carefully to their ideas instead of dismissing or overruling them. He also cautioned me about my impatience with people who I thought were not good at what they did or didn't carry their weight. I was not always very good at what I did—but I wanted people to tell me when I wasn't. I thrived on input. I was always curious about how people thought I was doing, and not about whether they liked me (even though that would be helpful). I didn't always love the feedback, but I would be more nervous if I didn't get any feedback. So, I was surprised when I told Wayland that a particular employee wasn't very good and we should probably tell him, and Wayland cautioned me not to. He would do it at a more appropriate time and in a way that the person could understand based on the relationship they had. I tried to control my frustration. I really did. But then again, Wayland was just as impatient as I was, maybe even more. Because he had such high expectations of himself and the people around him, he got frustrated very easily, particularly with the senior people in the company.

I was particularly frustrated myself by one individual who I considered inept, which led to an invaluable lesson from Wayland about ability versus perception. After criticizing this person to Wayland and claiming that I could do his job better for less money and even without training, Wayland said I probably could, but that I hadn't earned the right to that job. I might be technically capable, he said, but the people in the organization would not respect me. In their eyes, I didn't have the gravitas, the knowledge, the experience, to actually do the job, and I'd spend as much time digging myself out of the perception hole as this guy spent sinking into it.

That made some sense to me, but I really balked at being held back due to my age. There was a job I really wanted, but Wayland said I was too young and hadn't earned it. "If I just sit here and exist and come back in five years, would you then give me the job?" I asked him.

"Of course not," Wayland said. "I'm not talking about you just sitting there and ripening. What I'm talking about is you seeing more, doing more, so that you can experience and therefore understand a lot more situations."

"Well, then it's *not* age, it's experience."

Wayland responded, "If you can get the experience over in five minutes, fine, but generally that's not the way it works. You have to live through things to earn credibility so that the people working for you will trust that you will get them through whatever challenge or crisis presents itself."

That was one of the many important lessons on leadership that I learned from Wayland. People turn their lives over to you when you're leading them on a big and risky project, and they have to believe that you have the experience to do it. So, though

I continued to agitate about my age, I learned a lot. It's amazing that Wayland and I were such good friends because we were so different and debated so many things from different points of view.

Paul Allaire, the CEO of Xerox, poached me from Wayland in 1991 to be his EA, evidently with Wayland's blessing. I was surprised. I'd challenged the CEO in a board meeting when he said for the umpteenth time that Xerox had a hiring freeze, which I knew was not true. "I'm a little confused, Mr. Allaire," I piped up from the sidelines. "If you keep saying we have a hiring freeze, and we hire hundreds of new people every month, who can say 'no hiring' and make it happen?" I shouldn't have spoken up, of course. My role was to sit quietly with the other EAs, but I just couldn't keep my mouth shut. Once again, I was summoned to the office of a top executive—this time *the* top executive. And once again I thought I was going to be fired. I wasn't. Instead, he offered me the new position. I was taken aback. "Why would I want to be your assistant?" I asked Paul. "Because I'm the CEO and I'm asking you," he replied.

As flattering as his offer was, I was reluctant to accept. I had already spent nine or so tough months working for Wayland, and the thought of setting off again as someone else's EA seemed a waste of time. I was not aware then of the value of being an EA to a top executive. It wasn't a permanent position, and I wanted to get back to a real job: being an engineer. That's what I had been trained to do, that's what I was good at, and that's what I liked doing. Besides, I didn't know Paul well. He was quiet in meetings and extremely different from Wayland. He was not always transparent, not that he tried to be secretive; he was just a quiet guy. *Why*, I asked myself, *would I go back and do this for a guy I didn't know and whose style was very different from what I was used to?*

Wayland had established a pretty notorious reputation by then as a hard-driving, work-work-work kind of guy, but I was used to him. *My god,* I said to myself, *I got through those nine months without killing myself, but why do it again? If I go work for Paul, will I start all over? And how long does he need me for?* But the bottom line was that I didn't know Paul, his style was so different from what I was used to, and I longed to return to my normal life.

It was Lloyd, yet again, who set me straight. There are many engineers at Xerox, he told me, and you are a very good one. But there is only one CEO, and he has picked you out of so many to be his executive assistant. You will learn things you never knew you'd learn and be exposed to events you cannot imagine. Who knows where it will lead? It's up to you, of course, but I think you'd be a fool to pass it up.

And so I became Paul Allaire's EA for two years.

The difference between Paul and Wayland was night and day. Wayland had come up through sales and had that big, extroverted sales personality, whereas Paul had come up through engineering and finance and was quite shy. Wayland had a million friends in the company; Paul had a small, tight circle he was comfortable with. Wayland was a workaholic, whereas Paul integrated his work with his family life and interests. (Occasionally he would leave work midday to go into the city to see the ballet.) Wayland was outspoken and volcanic; Paul was understated and incredibly calm. I remember his taking his blood pressure once, and it was something like 120 over 60.

Paul, too, gave me lessons in leadership, some of which were difficult for me. One was to give people credit for ideas that they didn't have by selling them my ideas and letting them have ownership. That was a struggle for me, but it turned out to be sage advice. The people with inherited ideas were far more apt to act on them. Another was the power of silence. Deliberately creating a silence to compel other people to talk was a very important lesson. Creating time for saying nothing puts the onus on other people, making them uncomfortable and causing them to fill the void. Paul was a master at that. I was not. My reaction to silence was restlessness and impatience. My instinct was to jump right in, take charge, and move on. Paul taught me the value of slowing down. He also counseled me often about controlling my emotions, my tone of voice, and my choice of language so that they wouldn't cloud the issue. I often got worked up about whatever the subject was, and people would get lost in my reaction instead of dealing with the substance. My bluntness had to be controlled, Paul said. I had to be very clear in an unemotional way so that the issue was naked and not blurred by my delivery. All were important but difficult lessons in leadership for me.

The most impactful tips I received were often not verbal, but experiential, and came from spending so much time first with Wayland and then with Paul and observing how they operated, how they thought, how they dealt with situations, how they handled work and family. It was my "immersive education," and though each man gave me verbal tips, the most valuable insights I got into leadership came from watching.

I remember going through one incredibly intense situation with Paul, which had to do with Xerox's insurance businesses, which had been brought on to diversify its interests. One of the company's business lines was reinsurance, which covered the risk of other insurance companies. We faced a string of pretty complicated insurance liability cases involving the health effects of building materials, which, if lost, would have created a financial crisis for Xerox. We could have lost the whole company, but Paul pulled us through. For months I watched him, an engineer through and through, methodically interrogate every detail of the problem with our team of lawyers, the insurance companies, and our financial executives; develop and analyze the various potential solutions; select the most reasonable path, and proceed to implementation. It was all done with a grace and a human touch that made it a true work of art. In the end, the company came out okay, and Paul was at the center of protecting the bottom line. I had a ringside seat to the pushes and the pulls, the positives and the negatives, and this unbelievable engineering-like approach to the problem and the solutions. I learned a huge amount from that experience.

Going through this crisis with Paul implanted in me the value of having a great team you can depend on, much like the loyal team of my mother's friends who looked out for us in our neighborhood. For the first time, I saw fully that a leader needs people around her who are experts, who know what the hell they're doing, so that the problem can be distributed in manageable pieces and get solved. I'm so glad I got to work with Paul before I progressed more in the company.

Paul died of cancer in February 2019 while I was writing this book, and I flew from London to Connecticut for his memorial service. He was eighty. I was struck at his service by one of the lessons I had picked up slowly during all the years I knew him:

the importance of consistency of personality. Paul Allaire was always Paul Allaire. He'd been brought up on a family farm in Massachusetts, and he died on his own farm in Connecticut. He became a very powerful man, but he never got too big. His identifiable traits never changed; he was always kind of silent, kind of a loner, an intellectual who never tried to be anything but who he was. I see now that he was more of a model for me than I realized at the time. He was a very good man and extremely important to Xerox—and to me.

I had to leave Paul in 1992, soon after I got pregnant with my daughter, Melissa, and my doctor ordered bed rest. When I brought her safely home from the hospital three months later, Paul flew to Rochester and was the first person from work to see her. I went on to work for Brian Stern, the senior executive in charge of the office copying division, but from the moment Melissa was born, I declared that I would not work on weekends or at night until the children were in bed. It didn't quite work out that way, but it was a good declaration for as long as it lasted.

One of my beloved mentors was Vernon Jordan, the civil rights veteran, a towering American figure, counsel and friend to President Bill Clinton, and a member of the Xerox board. We met in a hallway at Xerox.

"Young lady," he said.

"Who, me?"

"Yes, you," he said. "I am Vernon Jordan."

"I know who you are," I replied.

"And how is that?" he asked. I told him I'd seen photographs of him in the magazines my mother brought home from thrift shops. He asked me my name and what sort of work I was doing at Xerox—I was then working for Wayland—and after chatting a bit, we each moved on.

To my surprise, I received a note from him in the mail a few days later. "Read these books," he wrote. "Nelson Mandela's *Long Walk to Freedom*. Toni Morrison's *Song of Solomon*. W. E. B. Du Bois's book of essays." Why those titles? They had nothing to do with business. I'd already read *Long Walk to Freedom*, but I eventually bought and read the others. And that was just the beginning. Vernon gave me another assignment when I saw him next at a board meeting, where I sat on the side with the other executive assistants. During one of the breaks, some of the assistants, Vernon, and a few of the directors were chatting about why it was so difficult to actually stop the hiring. I, in my blunt and unpolished way, said that the situation could be fixed with a different, more direct approach. As we were reassembling for the meeting, Vernon said quietly, "Think about what you said and give me a call." I did think about it while I waited for the scheduled call time. Before we spoke, I realized that my comments were inappropriate for the group and the time. The thoughts by a junior observer should not in any way detract from the leadership team. As only Vernon could say when we spoke, "It is not about you." It was a lesson in teamwork, knowing your place, and respecting leadership.

Vernon, who was twenty-three years my senior, became a sort of godfather when I left Wayland to work for Paul Allaire. I saw him more often, and we sometimes traveled together. Vernon also stopped by for a chat before board meetings and occasionally followed up by phone afterward. One such call after a meeting concerned a certain individual being promoted to senior vice president. "What did you think of the guy?" Vernon asked. I responded dismissively with a familiar refrain: "I can do this guy's job for half the money." Vernon told me that my answer was about me, which is not what he was asking, and that I should articulate it from a business perspective. That was just one example of his coaching. There were many more as I moved up in the company.

At one point, when I was invited to present to the board on some subject or other, he chided me for wearing what he considered an "inappropriate outfit." Another time, he congratulated me for wearing stockings, which I rarely did. "Stockings should always be worn," his final note read, a directive that only he could have given me. But what he meant was less about attire and stockings and more about the importance of presentation. He was saying, in essence, "I want to make sure you understand you're visiting the board— you're not on it—and this place is different from your normal. It's a higher level, and people are judging everything about you. It's really important that you are aware of where you are." He wasn't criticizing me straight out but rather leading me to think through what he was suggesting. His was a fundamentally solid and good approach to coaching and mentoring. He was gently guiding me to fit the part of a corporate person, a part I had so religiously resisted. I liked looking defiantly different, having rejected the mini men suits and little ties that the other women wore. I had rejected straightening my hair and instead sported an ever-expanding Afro. I literally tried not to fit in, but I realize now, and probably did then, that my defiance was as ignorant as total compliance. The trick was to find the comfortable spot between the two, which eventually I did.

Vernon did more than critique my professional life. He broadened my horizons, inviting Lloyd and me to receptions and introducing me to his many contacts, one of whom was Bill Clinton. I was flattered, of course, but more than that he gave me the sense that I had something really special, that sometimes it was no longer worth picking fights to be different, that it just wasn't important.

Vernon straddled both worlds himself and mastered each beautifully. He was a corporate guy, and he wasn't really a corporate guy. He was of the establishment, and he wasn't. He had an aura around him that everyone recognized. He spoke differently, in the slow, measured cadence of a Black man from the south. He dressed differently, in impeccably tailored business suits and imported shoes. He would sometimes use curse words in board meetings, but coming from him, they didn't seem like curse words. He was totally comfortable in his skin, and he was teaching me to be comfortable with who I was. He was exceedingly generous, and not only with me.

I found out later that Vernon godfathered many other young people, white and Black, in the companies on whose boards he sat. One of his early protégés was Ken Chenault, who rose to enviable heights as the CEO of American Express. Vernon told me he treated his "students" the way he treated his own children and the interns he mentored as senior managing director at Lazard Frères, an investment banking firm. That's the kind of man he has always been, and I count him now as one of my closest and most treasured friends.

Paul Allaire also broadened my life, one time inviting me to accompany him and his wife, Kay, on a late-summer jaunt to Martha's Vineyard, where they were to have dinner with his friend Bill Clinton, the Democratic nominee for president, and attend various events. Vernon and his wife, Ann, were also part of the entourage. I was still Paul's EA, however, and had no idea what my role was. I thought I was just a tagalong and would be dropped off somewhere until the bigwigs were through, but no, it turned out that I was invited to attend some of the events, including one at the home of Katharine Graham, the publisher of *The Washington Post*.

I was advised to keep an eye on the Secret Service so I wouldn't be left behind when they moved the Clintons, and I followed that directive until my eyes ached. I was obviously the lowest in the pecking order, and no one was going to hold up the cars and say, "We've got to wait for Ursula." But there was ample time to behold the movers and shakers there, including Katharine Graham, who was an amazing woman.

I also attended a small dinner for Hillary and Bill Clinton. I had met the presidential nominee briefly before with Vernon and liked him enormously, but this was the first time I'd met Hillary, and I found her very impressive. I was seated at her end of the table and didn't engage her in conversation, being of such low stature among these powerhouses, but I listened as she talked about health care. She peppered the table with question after question about how many employees were covered, what coverage they had, what health insurance cost the company, and on and on. I was awed by her knowledge and professionalism.

Katharine Graham. Bill and Hillary Clinton. Vernon Jordan. I was struck by the people I was hanging out with that weekend. They were all amazing. They had come from different backgrounds, but they had many things in common: They had had strong parents and received a good education at top schools. They were well-read and curious and could understand complex problems and situations. They were all high achievers and had high expectations for themselves.

I love the phrase "Talent is evenly distributed. Opportunity is not." I don't believe you are born with greatness, though I think there are things that can prevent you from becoming great. I think you are nurtured into greatness, and the Clintons and Vernon were clearly nurtured to a very high level of performance and achievement. They were among many examples of nurtured individuals ending up being successful people. If you water a plant, it keeps growing.

I was especially fond of Bill Clinton, though I didn't ever work with him professionally. He was out of office by the time I became an executive in the company. I did hear him speak on many occasions, mostly at the White House, when Xerox was invited to participate on various subjects. I remember one such gathering at which President Clinton spoke to Black executives about equal opportunity. I went with my husband and Emerson Fullwood, a corporate vice president at Xerox, and was, as usual, very impressed by Clinton's talent as the "great explainer." His style was not to press his point of view on an audience, but to walk the audience through his reasoning, laying out the foundation for his position. At the same time, he exuded enormous warmth and charm, a winning combination for his proposed policies. I will always remember that dinner with him and Hillary and Vernon and Ann on Martha's Vineyard. I was a lowly fly on the wall then, taking it all in as my career was expanding.

As the CEO's executive assistant, I was tiptoeing into the executive suite. I was not there yet. When you are in that position, there are things the company knows about you—that you're pretty smart, that you've worked hard at a single task, and that you're fairly adaptable and can fit in without being a buffoon.

What you have not proven yet is whether you can parlay those attributes into a leadership role. Will people actually follow you? Can you build a team so you can work with others in a collaborative way? Can you follow as much as you can lead? I still had much to prove. But then again, I had Vernon nipping at my heels, urging me to make that jump: "You have to work harder, Ursula." "You have to be smarter, Ursula." "You have to bring people along, Ursula."

I don't think I was as ambitious for myself as Vernon was for me. I was enjoying the various projects I was working on, especially when Paul put me in charge of turning around our Facsimile and Office Color business. This small, $300 million business was losing $30 million a year. My job was to try and figure out a way to turn a profit. It was the first real business I ever ran, and the experience was instructive as well as fun.

The fax business was headquartered in Lewisville, Texas, so I went down there to see what was going on. I was being advised by a guy named Mark Waxenburg, who was far more a business pro than I was. "You always have to understand the fundamentals of how a business makes money," he told me. And so I put together a small Texas team from the hundred or so people in the fax business to parse every detail of their operation, particularly the useless color copier. Xerox had developed the first color machine, but we hadn't tested it in the market because it was so expensive that no one could afford it. The product line had been short-lived.

My team and I developed a first-year business plan, and I remember making what I thought was an unbelievably good presentation of it to Paul. We could turn the company around in two years, I told him proudly, expecting high praise. Instead, Paul sat there stony-faced, as only he could, and said, "Break even next year or shut it down."

Was I crushed that this great plan of mine might be doomed? No, I was exhilarated. Paul's direction was very clear. If we turned the business around, great. If we didn't, no problem. The business would no longer be in our portfolio.

I started spending Monday to Friday in Texas, leaving my children at home with my husband. I worked closely with Rick Bliss, my number two guy on the team, who knew a lot about the fax business, while I knew about where the business fit into the company's investment choices. Rick was a great partner to have on this mission to reduce costs. And slowly but steadily, my team and I did.

The business was a small part of a large company, and we found that it was burdened with big business processes and costs that it couldn't afford, so our first step was to take it out of Xerox and treat it like a stand-alone small business. We looked at every single line item of the profit-and-loss statement (P&L) and basically changed how we packaged and shipped the products, how we customized them, and how we priced them. We reduced the number of products we offered and removed some features to lower the costs. And we questioned why we assembled and kitted the machines in Texas and not at the suppliers' sites in Asia and Mexico.

Our initial work was focused on reducing costs, and then we moved on to increasing revenue. And it worked. The combination of lowering costs and bringing in a bit more revenue allowed the team to meet Paul's challenge of breaking even in twelve months. Moreover, in the following six months, we turned a profit of

$5 million! In addition, my team back in Rochester focused on revamping the color business strategy from top to bottom.

My knowledge of corporate processes and the relationships that I had developed during my stints with Paul and Wayland were invaluable during my first role managing a P&L. I was able to see the business through the eyes of the people who made the decisions on how to allocate capital and risk. The fax business was small and not very strategic to the company's future, but it was important that it not be a drain on the company. Breaking even gave the company time to determine its long-term future.

In addition, because I understood how things were done and who did what, I could get schooled by the best people on the best way to proceed in different situations. Paul was very helpful during that time. I spoke to him about what was going on in the business, and while he did nothing directly, just having his ear and discussing things with him was immensely helpful. It was like a kid who approaches her parents with a question, debates the options out loud, and then walks away saying thank you even though her parents never opened their mouths.

Taking hold of the facsimile business turned out to be a really great experience that taught me valuable lessons, like how to control the size of a team. Because the team in Texas was so small, it was tight and you could put your arms around the issues and the discussion. It was just amazing how much control I had, which would have been impossible in the larger sphere of our business. From that point on, I tried to keep the teams around me small enough so that we could have a single, quick communication, without a lot of matrix and hierarchy.

I faced some communication challenges, but nothing insurmountable. The pace in Texas is slower than in the Northeast, as are the speech patterns. I didn't slow down the rapid-fire way I speak, but I urged members of the team to put their hands up if I went too fast. Communicating with Texans, however, turned out to be a piece of cake compared to my next job, which involved Germans, Spaniards, Frenchmen, and Brits.

I was a long way from Texas, and again because of Paul. He'd decided that our European operation should be run from London rather than the US, and he sent me off to do it. Europe was our biggest customer base for our midsize machines, those copying from twenty-five to about fifty-five pages a minute, and Paul decided that Xerox would have more international strength if it led the business from Europe.

And so it was in 1994 that my husband and I packed up our kids and moved to London to run the European Mid-Range Copier Group. It was a much bigger assignment than Texas and a bold move on Paul's part. Xerox had sent another woman, Diane McGarry, to run marketing in Europe, but this was a new position and they'd never relocated a woman who brought her family along. My family and I lived happily in London for three years.

Running the European operation was challenging for me. I had to learn how to operate my first really large business group and handle my first really large P&L responsibility. I ran all of the development, the marketing, the product design. I was responsible for the marketplace and for employees who were living around the world—some in Europe, some in the United States, a few in Japan. And as if that weren't challenging enough, I had to do it all on my own from the UK, checking in periodically with my US management. It was a big job for a thirty-six-year-old, but also a major career opportunity. My time in Europe was extremely formative and instructive for both me and my family.

We lived in a big, wonderful, American-style house that a corporate real estate agent found for us in Hampstead Heath, a huge green space within London with playgrounds and walking trails. The house had an attic playroom, a stacked washer/dryer, and a typically small English dishwasher and fridge. The challenge was to get to the greengrocer every day before it closed because the English, for no apparent reason, did not believe in home deliveries.

The children were young when we moved—Malcolm, six, and Melissa, two years and ten months. We had a live-in nanny, Janet Utley, a Londoner who was wonderful with the kids but maintained a strict work schedule between Monday and Friday. She often went out with friends at night and home to her mother's house on the weekends. Janet came and went as she pleased, and that was fine with us. We didn't want her in our lives all of the time.

We enrolled the kids in school. Malcolm started in the first grade at the American School in London, and little Melissa entered preschool at the Eastside Preparatory School, where she wore a great uniform and learned French. Every morning either Lloyd, who continued to work as a research scientist for Xerox in England, or I delivered Malcolm to the school bus and Melissa to school, and Janet picked them up.

Maneuvering over the English roads was a particular challenge for me. I drove my car to our office in Marlow near Windsor Castle, chanting "Stay left, stay left" to myself as I negotiated the roundabouts (traffic circles). I pulled over to consult the A–Zed road maps of London in this pre-GPS era whenever I got lost, which was often. It was madness, really. There I was, driving around London when I'd never driven in New York City!

One of Paul's mantras about travel was "When in Rome . . . ," and we took it to heart. Lloyd and I went to the horse races at Ascot, and I wore a big, peach hat. We went to Bath with the children and to Brighton and Birmingham. We went to Wimbledon and Oxford and Cambridge and to Scotland to visit my friend Catherine Cronin in Dunblane. Our travels reminded me of my mother's insistence that we have experiences we hadn't had before to stimulate our curiosity. We did all the British stuff we could and had a wonderful time.

What wasn't wonderful was a tricky situation in the office, which involved a cigar-smoking Frenchman whose office was right next to mine. The smell of his cigar smoke gave me a headache and was, in fact, against the no-smoking-in-the-office policy Xerox had adopted for our locations worldwide. Most people in the Xerox building respected the policy and either smoked outdoors or somewhere where you couldn't smell it, but not this guy. The tricky part was that he was very senior and ran the European sales force. There I was, a young, Black American woman living in the kingdom of this respected man, challenging him about his long-established habit of smoking cigars in the office. He was incredulous at first, but he finally moved his cigar smoking somewhere else in the building, and we ended up getting along just fine.

I had some difficulty with another Xerox Frenchman I brought onto my work group copier team. He too had been around longer than I had and obviously knew this area of the world better than I did. He was an important member of the team, but it was very clear he didn't like the fact that I was his boss. He was always subtly undermining me and questioning my decisions, dropping a little reminder that there was something he knew that I didn't. It took me quite a while to understand that he had a personal problem that had very little to do with me. He simply thought that he should have my job.

This situation was not unique. Seniors in a company can wish to be somewhere else, and so can subordinates. This Frenchman was a senior guy in a subordinate position, and he clearly didn't like it. But in the end, so what? It was just one of those things a leader has to push through and keep going, making sure the aggrieved employee isn't placing a bomb in your team or sabotaging anything. In the end, he and I figured out a way to work together, even though our relationship was never very good. We stuck to business, and the relationship ran by the book. We never got to be buddies, but we were never really enemies either. I considered it a "neutral work relationship," a phrase I would use time and again during my career to describe a sort of positive standoff.

Sorting out personnel issues was just one of the strengths I honed during my time in London. I learned other lessons as well, like how to function well without the comfort of the familiar home office. I was on my own. From a business perspective, I had a huge amount of independence—setting plans to be in Spain one day, the northern part of London the next—and I really enjoyed that. The five-hour time difference with the US made conference calls challenging. I was often in the office alone until 10 or 11 at night, but I loved that feeling too. I gained confidence and maturity being so far away, and when it came time to return to the US, I didn't want to go. My three years in the UK were a vital building block to my eventually becoming the CEO. In addition, they strengthened our family and the relationship between me and Lloyd.

My three years abroad gave me a lot of experience others hadn't had. I learned that distance from the mothership is a great development opportunity. I learned that culture is a big deal and that not knowing a country's language is a significant disadvantage. You have to be very aware of that failing and respectful that you need help in interpreting what people say and what you say. And I learned the value of knowing world history. The Europeans are passionate about their histories and their relations with other countries.

How farsighted Xerox was to give me that opportunity to work abroad! It was a decision that didn't happen accidentally. Paul and Wayland knew that they had to give their employees different experiences so they could grow. An employee who has limited skills, has never worked outside the United States, and has never even been outside the work environment would never develop into a competent leader. And they knew that great experiences, combined with my potential, would increase my chances for advancement and would ultimately benefit the company. My time in London was thus very helpful for both Xerox and me.

Living abroad or just going away on a vacation often opens your eyes to how you are living at home. When we returned to Rochester, I looked around and said no. We were still living in the house that Lloyd had lived in with his first wife, and for me, anyway, it was "old." We started looking for a new house, and the one we bought, on Greenfield Lane, seemed like a palace to me. The five-bedroom, six-bathroom, six-thousand-square-foot house had been erected in the twenties, as had most of the houses on Greenfield Lane, during the boom years of commerce from the newly completed Erie Canal. Built originally in England, the house had been moved brick by brick to Rochester, along with the wood paneling adorning the downstairs rooms. It was a beautiful, beautiful, beautiful place, and it even had a swimming pool. We lived there happily for twelve years and only sold it when I became president of Xerox and had to relocate to Connecticut. The kids were also transitioning to college at the time, and we didn't need such a huge house. Rochester remained home, however, and we rented an apartment there where Lloyd spent much of his time.

Rochester itself was a pretty remarkable place. Though the commercial boom that followed the completion of the Erie Canal had faded with the advent of the railroads, there were many vestiges of Rochester's important past. Susan B. Anthony, who led the women's suffrage movement in the nineteenth century, lived in Rochester, as did the great Frederick Douglass, a former slave, abolitionist, and newspaper editor who was active in the Underground Railroad. Rochester was also home to George Eastman, who founded Eastman Kodak, and to Joseph Wilson, who founded Xerox. The city has several public parks designed by the famed landscape architect Frederick Law Olmsted, the designer of Central Park in Manhattan and Prospect Park in Brooklyn. Lloyd and I had originally planned to have a wedding ceremony in Olmsted's Maplewood Park among its three thousand rosebushes, but we got distracted by work and our marriage license expired. Who knew? Our second try succeeded, and we were married in Lloyd's living room, attended only by my husband's close friend, Roy Pinkeney, Lloyd's daughter, Marge, and his granddaughter,

Aja. A few kisses, a few photos, and the shrimp platter Marge brought. Perfect.

I was happy in our new house in Rochester and, in 1999, with my new job at Xerox: overseeing the manufacturing and supply chain as vice president of global manufacturing. I was young for such a big job, only forty-one, and the age issue came up as it had in every previous job at Xerox. Everybody around me was older, even people who worked for me in manufacturing. I never felt that people suspected I had "slept my way to the top," or that I had advanced because I was a woman or Black. It was more like, "Why are you here? What have you done to deserve this job?" But by the time I was put in charge of manufacturing, I had a long list of bona fides justifying my advancement. Paul and Wayland had been right about my need to gain experience, despite my impatience, and they had made sure I did.

At some point every day, I walked the floor of the factory in Rochester, a vast space longer than a football field, where we manufactured our large machines, some smaller ones, and almost everything that went into them. The finished machines were then tested and sold at our sites around the world and accounted for over 60 percent of the company's $8 billion in revenue. And it was all my operation.

The seven thousand or so union workers in manufacturing considered themselves the heart and soul of the company, and with good reason. They made the stuff that made Xerox, Xerox. They were highly skilled—and they knew it. That gave them a certain sense of superiority, and they were unimpressed with managers like me—which is why I walked the floor every day and stopped by various stations to talk to the workers. I don't know whether my predecessors did that, but I felt doubly challenged by being the first woman, and a Black woman at that, to run manufacturing. Several articles were written about me in the local newspapers, and it helped that they'd read them and learned that my low-income background was more similar to theirs than to that of a white male Ivy League graduate. It also helped that I was an engineer and understood the products and the process of manufacturing.

We were entering a tricky time with the union at Xerox. We were facing another round of stiff competition from Japanese copier companies like Ricoh and Canon, as well as from the US-based Hewlett-Packard, and our market share was declining. Costs were always a focus, and a whole new world was opening up as automation and outsourcing reduced the need for US workers on the factory floor. Both were a tremendous disruption to how we had always done business at Xerox. And it came to a head on my watch.

When I first looked into outsourcing, I didn't think it could work. I thought we had something that was so totally unique that nobody else could do it. We weren't manufacturing cars, which all have basic components like steering wheels and seats. Xerox products had proprietary or unique parts.

I was as resistant to outsourcing as was everyone else at Xerox, including the union and the engineers. For me, it was more a question of losing control. I relished being able to walk down the floor and have the most important parts of the supply chain under my purview. It was a big challenge to let go of that. But little by little we did, and our efficiencies significantly improved.

We were still using big handheld car phones, but it was no longer necessary to have a room the size of a mansion to house a computer. The pace of technological advancement had accelerated. The challenge for me, in the leadership of a technology company, was determining how we could keep up and how quickly we could change. It was a very tricky time.

The use of electronics was exploding in everything from automobiles and kitchen appliances to office equipment (no surprise there). Instead of a lot of mechanical controls inside the machine, we transitioned to using electronics and software to replace gears and pulleys. Our workforce was largely skilled in building things that were mechanical, and there was resistance to shifting to software, but once we started the ball rolling, our employees got it. And so did I.

I had to learn the new language of electronics and bridge the gap between Xerox's past and its future. We were not yet over the past, but the future hadn't quite arrived. Still, one change led to another—a robot replaced a human welder, a machine tested equipment instead of a human doing it—forcing us to transform a lot of our testing methodologies as well as the skill sets of the people on the line. Our design for efficiency was improving so rapidly that what we needed on the ground in the factories was changing almost every day.

In addition to managing all these technological changes inside the factories, my job was also to deal with opening and closing plants all over the world. Our plant in Salvador, Brazil, for example, made toners and photoreceptors and was too large based on the demand from that region, but we needed more capacity in North America and more capacity in Europe. The new trade and tax legislation coming to bear at that time made it attractive to open up plants in new places. Ireland, for example, became a very-low-tax country, giving us a lot of incentives to move work there, which we did, opening an assembly plant in Ballycoolin. My team and I handled all of that—running a factory, doing factory planning, adjusting the manufacturing and supply chain, dealing with the unions, and so on.

I was working my tail off and loving what I was doing, but the hours were creating a nightmare at home. The children were then eight and eleven, and the end of the workday always prompted a flurry of phone calls with my husband to see which of us was going to pick them up and where. The kids had outgrown their after-school programs and were now playing sports like volleyball and basketball and doing homework with friends all over the place. Lloyd and I had to figure out what to do. "We do not want to outsource the raising of our children," I said to him, and Lloyd stepped up to the plate. "I've been working at Xerox for forty-two years. Why don't I retire and stay home?" he said. It was a perfect solution for all of us, and I was grateful to him, as his retirement enabled me to continue working at the career I loved.

A large part of my enjoyment was my good relationship with Paul Allaire. Not many people were able to work as closely as I did with Paul, and this privileged relationship put me in a very good place. I had a really good relationship up and down the management team, and I felt valued.

Unfortunately, it didn't last.

CLOSE CALL

The clouds began to gather as Paul prepared for his retirement. The first person hired to replace him, Vittorio Cassoni, died tragically and very unexpectedly shortly after he was hired. The second, Rick Thoman, arrived from IBM and had worked for American Express and RJR Nabisco, a solid pedigree. He had never been a CEO before, but he was a business executive with a very specific mandate to streamline and modernize Xerox.

It did not go well.

Cracks began to appear early on. The sales force was thrown into disarray when Rick changed the approach from geographic coverage (i.e., sales personnel concentrating on customers by region) to a vertical industry realignment (i.e., sales personnel assigned to specific industry types). The idea was to transform the sales force into experts in banking or insurance or manufacturing, for example, and sell those customers not only Xerox hardware products but consulting services to help them increase their business operations. The purpose was to establish new, more substantive relationships with customers and tailor new machines and services to their needs.

The idea was not a bad one. Many companies were trying to adopt this model, as we did eventually. But Rick's implementation at Xerox was too quick and radical, and it backfired. Relationships are all-important in a high-value selling business, and customers complained about this "new guy" showing up when they wanted Joe, the sales rep with whom they had developed a relationship. Joe knew them, had coffee with them, asked about their families, and understood their special needs or circumstances. If something went wrong, even if the customer ran out of paper, he or she could call Joe and say, "Hey, I'm stuck," and Joe would respond. Relationship breaks were a huge problem in our company. Customers hated it when Xerox replaced their familiar sales reps—and this was especially true of the larger, more profitable commercial printers. Commercial printers are often small or family-owned businesses, and commercial printing is their life. "I just bought a $100,000 machine, and I want my old guy back," a customer would say. During Rick's reign, customers left us and sales dropped.

The cracks deepened when Rick tried to streamline Xerox's billing process. Xerox had billing centers in just about every major city all over the country—more than thirty in all—and Rick wanted to consolidate them into three. It was, at first, a worthy project. The multiple billing centers were a source of frustration for management and a source of inefficiency for the company, and we had been working for some time on a plan to consolidate them into a few regional centers. Our previous efforts had resulted in only minor improvements because the process was complicated.

We had very complex bespoke billing, charging the customers for every copy over a certain contractual number and for the material used. We had meters that recorded how much toner was used, how many blank pages, color pages, two-sided pages, etc., for every machine. The billing got more complicated if the customer leased multiple machines. The person assigned to the account not only had to gather the different meter readings but address the different plans the customer was on and reconcile the numbers. All of that required significant work on the back end.

The process was further complicated by the rate at which we were making faster and more complex machines, some producing 135 pages a minute. We had come a long way since our early 914 model printed fourteen pages a minute, black and white, one side only. Billing then was really easy, but it became more complex as we added new features to the machines and charged customers for the increased functionality. The complexity of the billing process required a well-thought-out plan before it could be automated or streamlined. That didn't happen.

We moved too quickly to consolidate the billing centers, against the advice of the people running the operations at the time. We also did not take into account the amount of time it takes for people in general, and especially veteran Xerox employees, to accept change, a critical lesson I took to heart. There was no doubt the math looked good, but we didn't explain the new process well or rally the employees behind it. Though the need for consolidated billing was obvious and we should have done it earlier, our approach was not the right one, and it did not work.

The atmosphere at Xerox was not positive, especially after the leadership realized the company was bleeding cash because of the botched billing center consolidation and falling sales. Despite the logic and strategic justification, the changes in the company were not working. This was not a well-managed project from the beginning, but a textbook example of poor planning and lack of attention to the culture of the organization. Then the situation began to worsen.

I'd heard about the cash-flow problem, but I was off doing my thing in manufacturing and wasn't involved. I was having my own separate issues with the new Xerox.

I met Rick soon after he was hired, and we seemed to hit it off fine. But our relationship soon soured. During reviews with the management team under this new regime, I started to feel that it didn't matter to the company how manufacturing performed. In the new Xerox we only seemed to be interested in doing it faster and cheaper. Sometimes it is useful when your management doesn't dig in too far, but when you're trying to implement large-scale transformation, the details and some of the nuance must be clear to everyone.

We never had an argument, never even debated, but my inter-actions with Rick during the year or so that he was CEO were not positive. My role in manufacturing the machines and engaging in sensitive negotiations with the union was definitely not high on his priority list.

His lack of interest in understanding the union's sensitivities was exposed during a trip we made together from Rochester to our factories in Webster, New York, to meet with the union leaders and the unionized workforce. Out of the seventy thousand or so employees at Xerox, approximately ten thousand were unionized, and almost all were in the manufacturing or distribution operations in Rochester. As head of manufacturing, the union was my responsibility, and the relationship between Xerox and the union had always been good. The person driving Rick and me was a union driver, and I'd cautioned Rick before getting into the car that we had to be careful not to discuss anything sensitive or specific because of that. So what did Rick do? He launched into a conversation about strategy with the union and our thinking about closing this or that factory—exactly what I had advised him not to do. I was flabbergasted.

He didn't seem to comprehend the bigger picture or include in his decisions the people in the management process who knew the risks that were involved. He was a white-collar leader with an aristocratic leadership style, which was so different from the blue-collar debate-and-consensus culture at Xerox. "It's okay sometimes to be ignored," I remember saying to one of my colleagues, "but it's not okay to believe that no matter what you do it won't make a positive difference to the company or to the CEO."

I did not have much direct interaction with Rick after that, but I was feeling less valued. I was in a bad place in the company I had grown up in and loved, and I began to contemplate a change. The job market was hot at the time for people like me—a proven executive with technical expertise and general management knowledge, and a Black woman to boot. Over the years, I had been courted regularly with offers from executive search firms like Spencer Stuart and Russell Reynolds for specific jobs on behalf of their clients, and each time I'd been totally fine saying, "No, thank you, unless you are recruiting me to run a major company." If the job was anything else, I wasn't interested. I was really happy where I was. Until I wasn't.

And that's when Dell called.

The headhunter offered me essentially the same job I was doing at Xerox, along with an upward career path, but the operation was very different. Dell was essentially an assembly operation, not a manufacturing operation, and its miracle of success was its supply chain. The company had perfected product personalization, creating computers to customer specifications cheaply and quickly. What Dell was doing was really smart, offering, let's say, five different keyboards, five sizes of memory, five different screens, and so on, and the company could pull it all together with materials from nearby suppliers. Dell was the first company to do this, and it transformed the computer sales industry.

Dell made its money upfront by optimizing the process companies call the "cash-conversion cycle," which was an enormous plus. Generally, companies like Xerox that made things stocked the products in their warehouses, shipped them to their customers when the orders came in, and then were paid. That means the money the company spent to buy parts, assemble the products, store them in warehouses, and so on was tied up until the customers paid.

Dell did it totally differently. Customer orders of components were fulfilled by its suppliers. The customers paid immediately, and then Dell paid the suppliers. The company's cash-conversion cycle was essentially infinite, meaning it could collect the cash before customers got their devices. No shelf time. No guesswork. In my eyes, it was a miracle business model.

The prospect of working at Dell was very appealing, even though we would have to move to Texas, so I went through the extensive interview process. I met with Michael Dell, the CEO, various senior vice presidents, peers, superiors, and a couple of subordinates to see whether I would fit in the organization. I filled out the Myers-Briggs Type Indicator questionnaire, which breaks down your personality traits, such as whether you're an extrovert or an introvert, how you process information and make decisions, and how you interact with the world (i.e., judging rather than perceiving). And I worked with the recruiter about where we would live in Texas, what neighborhood school would fit our children's needs, where we would feel most at home. That was a big deal to me—and to them. The last thing a company needs is to bring someone into an environment they hate, so companies work hard to maximize the chance of a good fit. Lloyd was okay with the job change, though neither of us was thrilled with having to move to Texas. Our feelings changed after we went to Austin twice to look at schools and neighborhoods the recruiter had recommended. We found we really liked Austin. Though we had never considered moving to Texas per se, Austin seemed to us to be a miniature NYC. So I hashed out the details—the salary, the title, the benefits—and accepted Dell's offer.

What I hadn't done was tell Xerox that I was leaving. My first, and I hoped, only call was to Hector Motroni, the head of human resources. He was stunned. "Have you told, Paul?" he asked. I hadn't, and for good reason. I was anxious that Paul, my old boss and now chairman of the board, would try to talk me out of leaving the company.

"You tell him," I told Hector. "That's your job."

But of course, I had to tell Paul myself, and a few days later I did. A prolonged silence followed my news. "Can you put everything on hold for a couple of days?" Paul finally said. "I'm going to come back to you soon." I agreed. That was easy enough. There was not much to put on hold. I had already taken the job with Dell, and I didn't think much could happen to change the outcome.

Then Vernon called, as both a friend and an important member of the Xerox family. Paul or Hector had obviously called on him to appeal to me as another member of that family, and he cleverly did not dangle money or position. "You cannot leave Xerox," he told me in that smooth, deep voice of his. "You should think about the company as a loyal partner you've been with for years, and then some young guy comes along and shows you flashes of greatness. And the reason you can't even think about it is because you have a great and steadfast partner who has stood by you through thick and thin and made you what you are. Now your partner needs you more than ever. We need you to stay."

I was puzzled by all the attention, and my question to Vernon and to Paul and ultimately to Hector was how my leaving the company could be such a big deal for them. "I'm not the CFO. I'm not the general counsel," I said. "I'm the guy running manufacturing, and you can find somebody else to do that." Where I had previously been feeling undervalued, I now felt overvalued.

I didn't know then the extent of the trouble the company was in or what was going on among the board of directors. I also didn't understand the high visibility I had in the company until Hector explained. People read signals very carefully when a CEO has been changed, he told me. Because I had always been considered to be dedicated to Xerox and Paul and the management team, if I left, it could be taken as a signal that the company had no hope, and that could be the start of an exodus of key people. "It would cause more damage than just what you're going to do," Hector said. "People would say, 'My god, Ursula's leaving. What the hell does that mean for me? I probably should leave as well.'"

I'd never thought about my departure from that perspective. I'd only thought about myself and my current unhappiness at Xerox, which is why a question Hector posed to me had such resonance. "Are you running away from something, Ursula, or running toward something?" he said. "Ask yourself whether you are running from Xerox or running to Dell."

Answering that question led to one of the most important lessons that I learned in this business. If you're running away from something, I realized, you are at a significant disadvantage: you sometimes compromise your principles, you take unnecessary risks, your emotions play a larger part in a decision than they should, and you become fairly selfish. I was guilty of all those things, and my resolve began to waver.

Hector clearly knew what was going on with the board of directors, though I didn't yet. "With the changes we're making, you are now, have always been, and will continue to be in a position to change the thing that you're running away from for the better," he said. "So, don't go."

And then Paul called with astonishing news.

Rick was leaving the company. Paul was coming back on as CEO. He was bringing on Anne Mulcahy, his chief of staff and a longtime Xerox colleague, as president and heir apparent. "Can you work with Anne?" he asked.

I'd known Anne for years. She was several years older and senior to me, and though we'd worked in different areas in the company—she'd been in sales and had headed HR—I liked her very much.

"Of course," I told Paul.

"Good," he said. "She'll need you, and so will I."

I called the people at Dell to say I wasn't coming, that given what was happening at Xerox the company wanted me to stay. "Got it" was their response. They were completely supportive, a real class act. "Give us a call if anything changes," they said.

I stayed at Xerox.

And the shit hit the fan.

WHAT DOESN'T KILL YOU . . .

The company was the definition of crisis in 2000 when Rick left, Paul returned, and Anne Mulcahy became a corporate warrior. Sales were way down because of the chaotic reorganization of the sales force. Our cash position had headed south because of the botched realignment of the billing centers; customers weren't paying because they weren't being billed or because they were contesting the charges. In addition to our self-inflicted wounds, we were being pressured by technology shifts and increasing competition. All told, we were entering a crisis of liquidity. We literally didn't have enough money to run the business. There was serious talk of declaring bankruptcy.

Anne would have none of it.

"Here's what I need you to do," she said to me. "Reduce costs in your part of the business by $2 billion." Two billion dollars! That sounded like a shitload of money, which it was, but a fairly large portion of the difference between revenue and profit—labor costs, material costs, tooling costs, overhead such as rent, energy, and more—was my responsibility. In 2000, Xerox had revenues of approximately $19 billion and approximately $2 billion of profit. "You own a major part of the cost," Anne said. "Go away and figure out how to reduce the costs without throwing away our future. We don't want to go through all this and have nothing left that makes us great, so please do it in a way that keeps the company whole and profitable, a company your children and mine would want to work for."

How straightforward can you get? Anne put on no airs, had no sense of superiority, no bravado, in what I came to theorize was a very female approach to leadership. "We're going to have to do this together because there's no way in the world I can do it alone," she said to me. "You know more about engineering, manufacturing, and supply than I do, and this is not going to be the normal role where I am the boss and you are the subordinate. That's not what we are doing here. You're the expert in this area. I'm the banker. Call me if you're stuck, and please yell if you're going to put the company at massive risk. But trust your instincts."

I thought at first that I could do it by myself, though I didn't have a clue just what to do, but I quickly discovered I needed help. I put together a team that included Betsy Rice, the CFO for manufacturing, who was key in pinpointing how any change would show on the P&L, and Clive Barons, who already worked for me in manufacturing and became a strong strategist. Clive and I discussed, debated, and recycled ideas that he or I or other team members came up with, and then he would go and model them. We also often benchmarked other industries or competitors.

I still had my regular job as head of manufacturing and couldn't really bring on others from my manufacturing team who had daily jobs to do, so I reached out to people who were deeper in the organization. Wim Appelo, who was working in our manufacturing operation in the Netherlands, became one of my biggest confidants. In addition to being fundamentally good at manufacturing management, Wim was very smart, a very strong strategist and organizational designer. He became part of my go-to team.

Reaching out to people who were not the next in line was vital to the progress that we eventually made. People at the highest positions, I discovered, didn't always have the best information, particularly when you wanted specific information about how things work or about how people feel. And we needed input from everywhere. To determine the size of reduction needed, we had to completely rethink what we did and how we did it. It was going to require a big change in the fundamental way we'd worked for years. We'd need untraditional ideas and had to utilize unusual people.

The prime example was Anne herself, the "accidental CEO" as she became known, who was definitely not next in line when Paul called her home to try to save the company as she was boarding a plane for Japan. She was a brilliant, if unexpected, choice, and we worked closely together for the next nine years as colleagues and friends. It turned out that we had a lot in common. I had worked only at Xerox; she had worked only at Xerox. I'd married a Xerox veteran; she'd married a Xerox veteran. Both of our husbands were much older than we were, hers by seventeen years and mine by twenty. We each had two children, though hers are a few years older than mine. We were both Catholic and both dedicated to saving Xerox.

My team and I started by looking at all our manufacturing

and supply chain costs. We examined everything: Where did we spend the money? People, machinery, taxes, transportation, energy, on and on. We looked at every type of cost, which informed us about the business in general and gave us hints about ways we could redesign the work process to make it more efficient. For example, we looked at the historic manufacturing buildings on our campus in Webster, New York, which were right across the street from each other and an easy walk. That seeming convenience was overshadowed by the transportation costs of making a machine in one building and moving it to another for testing, plus the time it took and the potential for breakage between point A and point B. We considered consolidating our manufacturing operations into just one or two buildings and selling the rest, but that wasn't likely to happen because no one wanted to buy them.

There wasn't a cost we did not consider, and we went through them, line by line, and investigated getting that service from some-body else or eliminating the work altogether. A useful tool in this exercise was benchmarking, which Xerox became well known for using. (Xerox learned and used benchmarking during our pursuit of the Malcolm Baldrige National Quality Award, which we won twice.) Benchmarking involves looking at businesses in your in-dustry and, if applicable, outside your industry, to find practices that are best in class and determining if and how each practice can be brought in house.

We asked ourselves a number of questions. How much can we save by moving work to lower-cost areas? Is there anything we can stop doing? Can we be more efficient? Then we categorized our findings as fixed or variable and high risk, low risk, or medium risk. It was very important that we reduce costs without taking

excessive or unreasonable risk. For example, it would be a
if we decided to assume higher productivity off the line from a
third party, booked all that productivity, and saved costs by closing
down a line only to find out we couldn't get everything we needed
from the outside. We had to avoid reducing the supply, screwing
up the quality, or delivering our products late.

Reducing the payroll was another major challenge. In 2000, we
had approximately ten thousand union employees. If I could get
total labor costs, including union labor costs, down by 50 percent,
I would save the company $1 billion. I presented that proposal
to the board of directors, along with our cost-savings proposals
from outsourcing. Though my ideas were well received, one smart
board member asked how I could implement the ideas when we
didn't have the right to reduce labor costs or make radical process
changes without union approval. Many union employees had a
work guarantee. Essentially, I needed the union's agreement to
fire its members.

One of the most valuable lessons I learned in my subsequent
negotiations with the union boss, Gary Bonadonna, is that if you
assume people are smart and that they can grasp the big picture
and make logical decisions, it is valuable to include them in analyzing the problem and designing a solution. And that's how I
approached Gary.

"I'm going to provide full disclosure," I said to Gary, a really
high-quality guy. "I am going to tell you the state the company
is in and everything that I know about the cost structure and
Xerox's profitability from the perspective of manufacturing and
the supply chain.

"I'm going to show you how we make money, and I need you to

help me, however you can, with the portion of responsibility that lies with you. We're already looking at ways to raise the prices of the machines. We're looking at ways to reduce taxes. We're looking at all kinds of ways to bring cost efficiency into the company, and I'm going to talk to you about the portion that you and I control. And that's manufacturing cost.

"Labor is a significant portion of the cost, so I know we are not going to be able to avoid discussing people. But I am willing to listen to anything else you suggest that has anything to do with reducing manufacturing costs. At the end of the day, however, I think we're going to come to the point where I will need your help in reducing the workforce.

"This is not about protecting my job or yours. We have thousands of people who don't have the same options that you and I have, and that's who we have to care for. My goal is to have as many people working for Xerox as long as possible in manufacturing, so you and I have to make smart choices.

"Here are the options. If we keep the current number of jobs, including union jobs, the company will go out of business in eighteen months, and then we'll have zero union jobs. Or we can cut a thousand jobs, the company will survive, and you'll have the remainder of the union jobs for the foreseeable future. Which is the better outcome?"

It wasn't as simple as putting some paper in front of Gary and getting his agreement. Naturally, I faced a lot of pushback. He did offer some concessions: "We'll outsource shipping but not the work of toolmakers because they're skilled, high-paid workers. We'll take a little cut in health benefits. We'll do anything to reduce the number of layoffs." It was a long, slow slog.

Our many discussions were always friendly, and we engaged in small talk about our families before we began negotiating. He didn't want to touch the welders and the toolmakers and especially the cleaning staff. We could have easily outsourced the cleaning and saved money, but he was adamant about it. There were other very specific things he wanted, like keeping on the short-distance Xerox truckers, a demand that I found puzzling, but after a while I realized he was dealing with opaque "union stuff," just as I was dealing with opaque "company stuff." We eventually got to the point where we didn't need to understand the inner workings of each other's area. We trusted each other enough to have confidence that we were each doing our best. His adamancy about an issue was enough for me to say, "Let's try another approach." He had to get the union to vote on the changes, and he knew a lot more about how to accomplish that than I did.

For the most part, we managed to avoid animosity toward one another, and our relationship never deteriorated. We did have one knock-down, drag-out fight over my ultimate goal to move a manufacturing plant to Mexico and Gary's determination to keep the plant and the jobs it provided in Utica, New York. Though the union and the company later agreed to close the plant, Gary was clear at the time that the proposed move was a line in the sand and, if we crossed it, he would have to consider a strike or a work disruption, so I backed down. A strike would have killed the company (we prepared a contingency plan for that), and so would a work disruption. If the workers on the line had sabotaged their own work, which is not an uncommon form of protest in some organizations, the company's revenue stream would have been destroyed. I was very aware of that possibility from my time walking the factory floor. If such sabotage occurred, we wouldn't have been able to fix it with the smartest of the engineers running down the aisles. But nothing like that ever happened.

Instead, Gary and I negotiated a new contract that included the overall reduction of the union workforce by some fifteen hundred, the reduction of work hours, and the relocation of work from Webster to our lower-cost factory in Utica, where the workers earned less. There were other concessions as well, and the new contract was approved. Gary and his union were engaged in the solution. It was a really big win for the company.

I believe that this give-and-take negotiating style is a particular strength of women. I managed to negotiate a compromise with the union that took into account the impact on people's lives and the community's viability, as well as the health of the company and the return to the shareholders. It was a balance that I had to reach, and I think, with the help of Gary and the board, we were able to get that done. Could a man have negotiated an equally successful settlement with the union? Probably, but the road could have been longer and rockier. There was no mano a mano between Gary and me, no winner-loser dynamic.

Outsourcing was another critical component of saving Xerox, though it came tinged with regret. My team and I visited at least three manufacturing plants in those early days of the outsourcing industry and chose Flextronics, an outsourcing company in California. I remember going to the board and proposing the move to Flextronics. That was a big deal for Xerox. We were proud of the fact that the company's scientists had invented our patented technology and that our engineers and manufacturing personnel made most of what we sold. Giving it up was a big adjustment for the company. Our culture revolved around our technology skills and the ability of our engineers and manufacturing people to work together and move a part a little here or a little there and solve an issue.

We had to feel very comfortable with the concept of our machines being built by people who were not Xerox employees. Even more than that, we had to fundamentally rethink who we were as a company. Since the rise of competition from Japan and the beginnings of competition from China, the salespeople had stressed to customers that we were an American company and that our machines were American-made by Xerox personnel. But that would no longer be true. (In actuality, we had already started down that road when Xerox began buying smaller products from our partner, Fuji Xerox.) Anne and I talked often about whether we were still a made-in-America company and what our message should be to potential customers. What would outsourcing mean to our value creation? Do we own this? We needed to rethink our approach and messaging. It may have been wrenching to have some of our products come from a third-party manufacturer, but it was the right thing, indeed the only thing, to do. We needed to reduce costs to increase profits and cash. This was vital for our ongoing viability.

So was the sale I orchestrated of a Xerox plant in Mexico to Flextronics. The sale made a lot of sense because we had too much manufacturing capacity in this new age of outsourcing and automation.

The move to Flextronics turned out to be a very good one. We lowered cost, delivered equal or higher quality, and didn't miss a beat in delivery. It was a triple home run that saved the company $250 million. Michael Marks, the CEO of Flextronics, became a really good business friend of the company. Flextronics increased our capacity and, over time, implemented new world-class processors, bringing us additional productivities and advances in technology. Xerox benefited by basically riding on the back of Flextronics' expertise, and many of our engineers ended up working for the company.

To decrease other personnel costs, we had layoffs across the board. The union workers were not the only employees affected. Everyone was—managers, engineers, manufacturing people. We accomplished the reduction through early retirements, contract buyouts, and simple job termination. For some older employees, taking early retirement was a bonus because their pensions were about to kick in. Union workers who were informed that their contracts would not be renewed were incentivized to leave early with the offer of a lump sum.

Working out the formula for the layoffs was a long and arduous process. The laws around the world prescribe what you can and can't do; in many countries you have to work with workers' councils (essentially unions) and get an agreement to reduce the number of people. The United States had different rules that revolved around discrimination and the protection of any group from disparate harm. The pain had to be shared—male, female, young, old, minority, white, married, single. The managers made the selections based on performance over the years. Generally, the lower performers went and the higher performers stayed, but then we had to look at the total picture. Was one group taking too big a hit? The big issue at the time was age discrimination. The inclination in every industry was to lay off senior people because they were paid more and presumed to have fewer modern skills. The numbers continued to grow over time and the government stepped in and made age discrimination illegal. Other groups were protected as well. If a company laid off too many African Americans or Hispanics or women, it would risk accusations of discrimination, so we took a long look at the total package of layoffs just to make sure it was balanced and didn't have a disproportionate impact on specific groups. While the process to comply with the government needs are complicated, the protections against discrimination are appropriate.

We did everything we could at Xerox to ease the anxiety of the people being laid off. Health benefits are usually contractual, but our severance packages went way beyond that by offering outsourcing benefits, retraining benefits, and outplacement assistance— none of which was required. We had professional counselors at layoff locations to work with the people being fired and with those who were left behind. We gave some employees money for retraining, depending on their skill sets.

We also looked at special situations, like a married couple who worked in the same facility at Xerox. Unless there was a performance issue, we tried to avoid laying off both family members. Even if we needed to eliminate both positions, we looked for ways to keep one parent employed. On the other hand, we had to be very careful about that because one person's compassion can be another person's discrimination. While we would have loved to be able to say, for example, "If you're sick, we won't lay you off," or "If you're a single parent, your job is secure," all of the healthy employees and childless workers would object, arguing that they were being discriminated against for not being sick or for not having a family. It may sound crazy, but after you get into it, you realize that such decisions would in fact be discriminatory and very difficult to justify.

Anne and I spent a lot of time thinking about the human impact of our decisions. It was her nature, as it was mine. I personally knew more than a few people in every layoff, and it was always very difficult. The employees were not being fired for cause but had been made redundant because their jobs were displaced by technology or because we'd stopped a whole product line or moved their work to another location. It was even difficult to lay off people I didn't know personally because I understood that we'd be changing their lives, at least in the short term, for the worse.

Laying off people who lived in Rochester, which is where I lived, was a particular challenge for me. Some of them had grown up in Rochester, the longtime manufacturing and engineering headquarters of Xerox, and had a very good standard of living. I knew they were going to have a hard time finding comparable jobs.

Inevitably, I got threats, but there wasn't much we could do about it. Our beautiful one-hundred-year-old house had a long driveway along the back of the property, and it would have been easy for anyone to come up that driveway without being seen. I remember the security team coming by and saying, "Your house is wide open, and this is not good." After a while we installed a security system, but I never felt that I or my family was in real danger.

This intense period lasted two years. My last waking thought every night was about Xerox, as was my first thought every morning. I learned then that the idea of work/family balance simply did not and could not apply. I was completely unbalanced when it came to my family life, but the sacrifice was necessary for the company to survive. I made a point of always being home over the weekends, but other than that, my husband was in charge of the household and the kids, who were then nine and twelve. We just did the best we could. I would be late for dinner or not show up for dinner at all, and my husband covered the bases. Without that support at home, there was no way I could have delivered what Xerox needed from me.

In the midst of all this, I had a hysterectomy. I had a history of uterine fibroids, which had sent me to bed rest during my pregnancy with Melissa. The doctor told me then that the tumors in the walls of my uterus were too large to be cut out and that eventually I would have to have a hysterectomy. I had put it off for as long as I could. The surgeon had to take everything out. I worked from my hospital bed and from the couch in my living room until I could return to the office.

There were constant meetings with Anne and the management team and the board of directors. What we were doing was vital, and we had to keep focused and moving forward. The Xerox family came together and supported each other.

Anne was amazing throughout all of this. There are some people you can count on for just about anything, and she was one of them. She was a brilliant manager of people and invested time and energy into buoying the spirits of everyone in the beleaguered company. She even gave employees the day off on their birthday.

Her first move as CEO had been to embark on a ninety-day mission, talking to customers and employees. She was rarely home with her family, instead circulating among the many Xerox sites, cheering on the sales force, meeting with customers, and haunting the banks to loan us the money we needed to get through the crisis.

Slowly, Xerox began to recover. By the end of 2001, almost two years since my first crisis meeting with Anne, Xerox once more started making a profit at the operating level. The personnel cuts had been draconian—nearly nineteen thousand employees laid off. Our costs, most of which belonged to me, were down by $1.2 billion. We could at last exhale. And I had changed. Where before I'd been more of a loner, I'd gained a different appreciation and respect for others, particularly some of my team members. Clive Barons, who became a personal friend, was smart and analytical while also being steely and aggressive; Wim Appelo, who was then head of strategy in our European operations, was a very good global and expansive thinker and went on to run all of manufacturing at Xerox; Frans Stollman was our nuts-and-bolts person who knew the details of how the crazy and relatively obscure parts of the company worked. Even Gary Bonadonna, the union leader who did not work for us, proved that he was an excellent businessman both locally and globally and a good thinker. The entire team showed me they could work twenty-four hours a day, seven days a week, with the tenacity and the perseverance needed to work through problems. The crisis had backed us against the wall, and we'd come through it together.

People often show their strengths during the worst times, and we definitely had that at Xerox in 2000 and 2001. From the cleaner all the way up to the manager, you saw the best in people. Even employees who were involuntarily leaving the company acted generously. In a drawn-out process, we closed our small, relatively un-

important plant in Utica. In two months or so, we had to move th
supplier from point A to point B and back up everything, while we
steadily reduced the employee count from one hundred to seventy
to fifty and then to none. We worried about people sabotaging the
plant or doing shoddy work, but they never did. We had always
shown them appreciation and respect, and they returned it.

The crisis was also a time of personal growth for me. I had
proved to myself and others that I could operate in very complex
environments and under pressure, that I was a reasonably good ne-
gotiator and a damn good communicator up and down, and that
I could integrate very complex sets of tasks into implementable
plans. I also found that I was pretty good at leading people and
that although I might be an unconventional, fearless person, I
wasn't reckless.

Much of this I suspected about myself, but I couldn't know for
sure until I was put into a tough situation where I had to prove
my value by actually getting the job done. I had always thought of
myself as being brutally impatient and extremely decisive. These
were strengths I had depended on in the past, but during the
crisis I learned that these attributes had to be tempered. I also
learned there is no substitute for facts and the truth. Humans are
generally resilient if they know what the reality is and have some
idea what the future is going to look like. In the past, I had occasionally tried to take a short cut and just get on with it. During
this experience, knowing that we had to go deep into the facts
with many people, I learned to slow down and give others time
to understand the details.

Anne and I made a particularly good team, even though, or
maybe because, we had expertise in different areas. We needed to

fit our skills together, and we did. The company exited the crisis stronger than before, and so did I. My role in helping Xerox survive had brought me once again to the attention of the board and had earned me new respect within the company. I had proved my mettle to others and to myself.

I could run this place, I remember thinking.

WOMAN POWER

Many stereotypes are applied to professional women: Women don't work well together; they will undermine each other. They can't be trusted. They are too emotional or, conversely, ice queens. They only got to the top by favoritism. They're a bad bet because of the distraction of children and family. They're weak. They're less likable if they express anger (consider Michelle Obama, who had to soften her public remarks on the campaign trail after she was dubbed "an angry Black woman"). On and on it goes. Really?

Anne and I were referred to in the press as the "dynamic duo," and that we were. We worked together for nine years, determined first to save Xerox and then to make it grow and keep it relevant and profitable in a rapidly changing world. She was CEO and I became her wingman, first as president of Business Group Operations and then as president of the company. We didn't operate in the traditional and strict reporting hierarchy. That wasn't Anne's style. We divided up between us and our respective teams the many tasks and challenges facing Xerox. We had proved ourselves during the crisis by helping to bring Xerox back from near death—and together we were spearheading the future.

I was made president of Business Group Operations (BGO) after the crisis and was responsible for most of the inner workings of the company—the engineering groups, research and development, product development, manufacturing, supply chain, procurement, information management—everything except legal and finance and sales. At first, I probably had forty thousand people working around the world, which would have made the organization chart seem daunting save for the fact I had an excellent team. Leading, I'd learned, is about integrating, not dividing. It's about putting it all together and knowing where help is needed. You cannot be a good leader without having a great team you can depend on to help lead.

Anne was the quintessential leader for all of us, and she and I basically ran the company hand in hand. She was Ms. Outside. A salesperson by training, she was very comfortable being the face of the company. She represented Xerox with governments around the world and with members of our own government; she was the major person in front of our board of directors, in front of Wall Street, in front of all our investors and large clients, and especially in front of our employees. I, on the other hand, was Ms. Inside, making sure the company, including my old territory of manufacturing, was running relatively smoothly. It was a role that was very comfortable for me and, I believe, for Anne.

We worked together on what needed to be done to run a company. We bought two small businesses, one in legal services and the other in mortgage services, to offset our reliance on copiers. We conducted a massive renegotiation of our partnership agreement with Fuji Xerox, which was very stressful and risky for the company. And even though she was stepping down at the time, we worked together on the major transition to services by acquiring ACS.

We worked separately as well, in what was probably an unorthodox dynamic. Instead of my reporting to her on every detail of what she'd assigned me to do, we split the responsibilities between us. I was involved in just about everything. I was part of the management team and sat around the table with Anne and the other team members. I felt as though I were her partner. It was personal.

Anne and I met independently, but not on a rigid schedule. When I led BGO, I worked and lived in upstate New York and Anne worked and lived in Connecticut. Often I'd communicate with her by email. We had a strong, symbiotic, and productive business relationship founded on trust and shared experience. I was part of her turnaround team, and we led the company together, grooming it and transitioning to services.

Anne and I bonded first as working mothers talking about our children. Her eldest son is two years older than my son, and her youngest son is four years older than my daughter. I soaked up everything she said about her children, as it helped me understand what to expect with my own. I remember agonizing to her about whether to give my teenage son a car. All the kids in our circle, the children of my peers, had cars. A car was the only way you could get around Rochester, but I resisted. We had raised our children to work for whatever they wanted, like a new game, by doing tasks around the house. They had to engage and participate as much as they could to earn their allowances, and there was no way my sixteen-year-old son could contribute in any meaningful way to a car, let alone the resulting expenses like insurance or even gas. No way were we going to buy him a car, I told Anne on one of our car trips. "Why not?" she asked.

Because my husband and I weren't raised that way, I told her. Lloyd's parents had given him room and board, clothes, and a great education, but for anything else he had to work. I had to work as well to cover my personal expenses. A car had never even entered the imagination. "It's ridiculous," I told Anne. "Malcolm can't begin to afford it." And Anne set me straight. "First of all, Ursula, you're in a different physical environment. You could take a bus or a subway in New York to get where you wanted to go, but Malcolm can't get anywhere unless you drive him. And two, you can more than afford to front the car for him. You're trying to raise your kids as if they were poor like you were instead of raising them as good rich kids who understand their responsibilities."

She was right. It was a great lesson. And she gave me another when I was bemoaning how that same son had gone merrily off to college without looking back, to which Anne said: "Then you've done your job as a parent." She softened her tone and added, "You can always call him just to hear his voice."

Still, our relationship was more professional than personal. We didn't socialize often outside of work, though we each had apartments on the upper east side of New York and often drove to the city together. We didn't call each other to chat as close personal friends do or go to the gym together or out to dinner often with our husbands. Our relationship was more purpose-driven as Xerox entered one crisis after another.

Just as Xerox was beginning to recover from near-death in 2002, another crisis threatened disaster when all the major ports in California were shut down in a dispute between shipping companies and the longshoremen's union. Most of our manufacturing components came from Japan, and our supply chain was on the brink of coming to a halt. Slowdowns and strikes were not uncommon and were always a headache, especially after 9/11, when new, stricter regulations were imposed on imports, but this ten-day strike was particularly damaging, coming as it did when we were still very vulnerable. We could barely afford the disruption of our supply chain and, by direct implication, our revenue and customer confidence. Orders for our machines went unfulfilled, deliveries were canceled, and revenue dropped.

We were not the only company suffering from the stoppage. So were many other businesses across the country, leading President George W. Bush to invoke the Taft-Hartley Act for the first time in twenty-five years. The ports were forced to resume operations, but there was a huge backlog of imports on ships still offshore and on the docks, creating even more delays. The good news, if you can call it that, was that our competitors were also handicapped by the strike, so we did not lose our competitive edge. The reason we survived was that everybody else was going through the same thing.

At least the economy was reasonably strong at the time. There were no external threats impacting businesses, like war or ecological disaster or the current pandemic, which is shutting down most commerce and travel and severely curtailing business consumption, energy consumption, personal consumption.

Just as we were recovering from the strike, we faced a new crisis as digital imaging and scanning and saving to memory began to take off. One section of our business benefited from that: our color copiers were being used to make prints of digital photographs, and our larger format color copiers were producing promotional and selling materials like beautiful brochures for new cars. But while our color copier business was growing nicely, other sections, like those producing billing statements and printing government forms, were rapidly declining.

For years, Xerox had virtually owned the billing business. Our super-fast, high-quality billing machines kept track of all the data on millions of pages and ensured, for example, that your detailed American Express bill was inserted in the envelope addressed to you. But those machines were now becoming redundant, and that aspect of the business was declining at an accelerating rate. In response, we doubled down on increasing our services offerings, the largest of which was document outsourcing.

Companies, large and small, had gotten into the practice of having significantly more equipment than they needed on their premises. Most administrative assistants had a small copier, a fax machine, and a printer near their desks. Every executive had at least one of these machines in his or her office. Most companies also had many medium-size "walk-up convenience" machines sprinkled throughout the building. That model worked for a while, but as the need for black-and-white copying declined, having all of this equipment sitting idle became an obvious sore point for customers. And it was quite inefficient and expensive for us as well. We stocked parts in warehouses and employed service people to take care of these underused machines. We solved this situation by developing a business offering called "document outsourcing."

Basically, we went into an organization and did a time-and-motion study for documents. We found out how many color and black-and-white copies the company made a year, and how much scanning and faxing each workgroup did. And we presented the company with a package deal that would result in higher efficiency and better overall cost. We told them, "We'll manage all your documents for you. We'll buy your machines, and you'll pay us for taking care of all your printing, copying, faxing, and scanning needs. We will be responsible for all your office equipment, whether it's from Xerox or a competitor. We'll manage everything for you, and all you have to do is pay for the document management services you use."

The service took off like wildfire. And the reason why it was really valuable for us was that a lot of the machines we took over were not ours. We were not a large supplier of small printers, so we actually took over the management of other companies' small printers and consolidated them and their copying and scanning functions into midsize Xerox copiers that were strategically located around the offices. We even took some machines out of a company's offices altogether and moved them off premises to various centralized sites and delivered the output to our customers. This proved to be very popular in big cities like New York and London and Paris, where real estate was very expensive and dedicating big rooms to copy machines was a waste of money.

Document outsourcing turned out to be a genius idea—and highly lucrative. The service allowed our customers to benefit from increased efficiency and decreased cost. It also allowed Xerox to become a strategic partner to our customers, a true win-win. Now all printer and copier makers do it, but at the time the services we offered were brand-new and very profitable. In truth, we invented the business.

Not all projects were such smooth sailing. I stumbled a few

times, once in a negotiation with Fuji Xerox over the pricing of our machines to them and theirs to us. My strategist, Clive Barons, and I had settled on what we considered a perfect price structure for our give-and-take with Fuji Xerox. We were to meet with them in Hawaii. But what we thought was the greatest solution in the world wasn't.

Clive and I went into the meeting with what we thought was the perfect solution. We told the Japanese that not only was it the obvious answer but that if they didn't accept the proposal today, the offer would be off the table. Afterward, we patted ourselves on the back, convinced we had succeeded in making clear what we needed, and they had not objected. And it had only taken us three days.

What we thought to be our triumph collapsed almost immediately when our Japanese cohorts informed us that although they hadn't objected to our proposal, they hadn't agreed to it either. I realized I had forgotten, or ignored, the basic tenets I'd learned about leadership: slow down, explain the change to the people it will impact, give them time to absorb it, and, as Vernon said to me so often, bring the people along with you. We hadn't given the Japanese any time to fully understand our proposal and to respond or express an objection. It was Ursula Burns running over them and just telling them what to do and expecting them to do it because it was obviously the right solution to the problem. This tendency of mine to overcontrol was not new. It almost always failed, including with my kids, so I'm not sure why I continued to do it. But the Japanese called me on it, and rightly so. In the end, what I'd thought had been accomplished in three days in Hawaii took three months to get done.

Japan wasn't our only international involvement, though Fuji Xerox was our most important partner. Xerox did business in 160 countries, and one of my many responsibilities was to make sure that each country had the machines and service parts it needed. It was often a thankless task.

Each sales team was responsible for ordering the specific items they needed to meet their sales forecast. We would respond, only to find out later that their projections had been wrong and we had sent too little or too much. Every field executive—the head of Xerox Europe, of the US, of developing markets—would yell, "Where the hell are the service parts? We needed them over here on Tuesday, and you didn't deliver!" And my team would yell back, "The problem is that you didn't sell what you said you were going to sell!" We were constantly bombarded. "All shit runs downhill," I used to tell my team, "and we are downhill." But it was more than an annoyance: we were missing revenue projections as a result. The multifaceted solution involved building more supply chain flexibility, using some predictive analytics, and working much more closely as a team, which finally reduced the yelling.

Despite the occasional glitches in our supply chain, our business outside the United States was doing very well and generated a growing percentage of our revenue. The globalization of business was not new. Every major American corporation has had manufacturing locations and employees all over the world for many decades. For companies that sell hard goods, it made sense to manufacture products closer to the people who were going to consume those goods. The market for US goods was also expanding as the world's economies grew and boosted more people out of poverty and into the middle class. Wealthier people consume more of everything, so naturally companies try to sell their goods on a global basis to as many customers as possible.

But there was a growing backlash. Globalization was blamed for the loss of American jobs, though automation and technology contributed heavily. Other countries also increased their capabilities and produced successful alternative or competitive services. Automobiles and airlines are great examples. Countries like Brazil and India are now producing their own cars and planes for their counties and other consumers. All that put pressure on jobs and wages in the US, and the push became to buy products made in America. It was fine to sell products overseas, just as long as they were made in America and therefore promoted American jobs.

That was one of the issues Donald Trump got elected on. His "Make America Great Again" campaign slogan recalled a time when America was an even greater superpower and made the products that people bought worldwide, helping to make America the largest economy in the world. And that message resonated. We were often asked, "Are you an American company?" The implication was that we would be better liked if we were. Some government contracts even mandated preferential treatment for American companies. Our answer then, and always, was that we were an American company doing business globally. We were fully incorporated and registered in the United States. We never considered ourselves anything but an American company. It was crazy to think that we could or should operate a company with our eyes focused only on the US. But there was pressure.

"Why do you have research centers in France? Or manufacturing plants in Mexico, Brazil, and Canada?" asked US government officials, senators and congressmen, state and local representatives.

"Why do you employ people outside the US?" Having only US-based employees would have been fine if we sold our goods and services only in America, but such a strategy would have been shortsighted. If we limited our potential customer base to the US, that base would have been 320 million. Worldwide, we had 7 billion customers, and that market was growing much faster than the US market. We had to serve the world to be successful as a company and as a country.

Overlooked in the "America-only" argument is the importance of exporting American business values, including intellectual property rights, workers' rights and protections, transparency, environmental responsibility, diversity, and inclusion. The countries where we had a presence did not necessarily align with those beliefs (and America doesn't always either), but this value set was the baseline for Xerox. Our employees in Russia, Africa, and South America were being introduced to a distinctly American form of business. It always seemed to me that the US government should be really happy when US companies export to the world not only our goods but also our values.

Operating globally was also economically sensible. We had customers in France, for example, so why should we make the products in America and transport them to France? We sold copy machines all over Europe, so wouldn't it be logical to make some of those machines in Europe? It was financially viable, reduced currency risk, and saved shipping costs and import duties. In short, it was good business, but the criticisms grew louder.

This debate intensified under the Trump administration. Apple's manufacturing base for its most popular products is in China, and the company stood to be hit hard by Trump's trade war with China. Trump's reaction? "Make your products in the United States instead of China," he tweeted. "Start building new plants now. Exciting!" General Motors was also on Trump's hit list when CEO Mary Barra closed a money-losing plant in Ohio and opened a new plant in Mexico. General Motors "has let our country down," Trump tweeted.

Trump was not the only US president to try to keep jobs in America, but he was certainly the noisiest. Anne had discussions with President Bush and I talked with President Obama about the same issue. The debate continues.

What is not debatable is that corporations are the embodiment of the capitalist structure. Corporations represent shareholders, parties who are interested in funding an idea or backing an investment. They represent the consumers of the products and services of the corporation. They represent the employees, the makers. The role of the corporation has always been to develop a business that will give investors a return on their investment. In the past, achieving that return has sometimes involved the neglect of workers who were too young or too poor or too vulnerable to complain about the lack of safety standards. As time went on, workers and communities got a greater voice, thank goodness, often backed by unions and governments that were embarrassed by fires in garment factories or miners trapped in collapsed mines.

We are living right now though another skirmish between the engines of capitalism and the consumers and by-products of capitalism. This one was started by a series of events coming together—the growing strength of women's voices in the Me Too movement, of minority voices in the Black Lives Matter movement, and the COVID-19 pandemic, which has turned capitalism and education on their heads. The pandemic has revealed the growing inequality of our world, where smaller and smaller percentages of people own more and more of the world's assets, and the failure of governments to be strong voices on behalf of their citizens. Governments in the United States, Great Britain, Brazil, Russia, and China, among others, have become more autocratic and more like monarchies than elected or representative bodies. The combination of all of those things is laying the foundation for yet another sea change in capitalism. There is greater discussion now about inclusive capitalism, a global movement to engage leaders from the business, government, and civil sectors to identify and support policies that extend the opportunities and benefits of the capitalist system to everyone.

Life was calmer in 2004, when I was invited to join the board of American Express while I was still president of BGO. That was a major opportunity and an unexpected honor. It was rare for anyone other than a CEO to be asked to be on the board of one of the top ten companies in America. American Express, a storied corporation with a unique business model, had had consistently excellent leadership since its founding in 1850. My surprise appointment to the board catapulted me to a different position in the business world.

My leap over the normal path to appointment was made possible by Vernon Jordan, a member of both the Xerox and American Express boards, and Ken Chenault, the widely admired CEO of American Express, who had also been mentored by Vernon. Vernon, who knew my record at Xerox and knew I could be on track to lead the company, had championed me to Ken as a board member. I didn't know Ken personally, but I certainly knew a great deal about him. He had a stellar reputation as an outstanding businessman and person.

Ken took a risk on me, but risk was part of his DNA. He was one of the true titans of industry. He grew up at American Express, and after twenty years with the company was made CEO. He served in that position for a stunning seventeen years (the average term for a CEO at that time was around five years). And he transformed the company. Cash had become less important in the 1990s as more payment instruments were being introduced. Customer loyalty programs were growing in popularity, and American Express was at the heart of the new and highly competitive benefits and partnerships. When I joined the welcoming and fairly diverse board, the company was solid but changing, and my comfort with change made me a good fit.

I had served on several boards before American Express, but of much smaller businesses or nonprofit organizations. My first company board was the PQ Corporation, a privately held company in Philadelphia started by Quakers. Among other innovative products, PQ made silicate retroreflective beads for traffic lane striping and detergent zeolites. The board work was defined by committees, and every board member served on all the committees—audit committee, compensation committee, governance committee—so I learned a lot at PQ. It was a perfect board to start with. The company was well run and had a positive culture.

A board's culture is important for board members to understand, as it determines whether they can contribute successfully. Culture encompasses the unwritten norms of the group. It is not found in the governance manual, and it does not define how the board members operate or what they think is important. The ideal culture, in my opinion, is one that is inclusive and open, a culture in which everyone's ideas are heard. And I was lucky to find that culture at PQ.

The board members worked well together, and I fit right in. I was an "expert" in manufacturing, had a strong technical background, and added value to the board from those aspects. I was on that board for eight years, including three while I was working in London; I had to fly back to the US four or five times a year for board meetings. Xerox was very supportive. At Xerox, managers, including the CEO, had to obtain approval from their corporate structure to serve on the board of an outside company. In addition to the positive aspects of being on a corporation's board (the prestige and compensation, for example), there are some negatives. Boards take time and present possible reputational risks. PQ was perfect. There was absolutely no conflict with Xerox. The time requirements were acceptable. And the board position was also useful because it helped me get more insight into how governance works in companies. It was a win-win-win situation for Xerox, PQ, and me.

I'd been invited to join the PQ board by a business acquaintance, Bob Rock, who I'd met several times at manufacturers' roundtable events. He was also an investor in PQ and called me while I was working as Paul Allaire's assistant to ask if I'd join the board. It was rare then for an executive in my position to be on the board of a public company, but I accepted. It sounded very interesting to me and was a major breakthrough.

Boards are a lot like clubs, even though this is changing now.

You generally have to know a member to get in. Members of one board are often members of another, which is how I was invited to join the board of the Hunt Corporation, also in Philadelphia, which made pencils and pencil sharpeners, among other products. From there I joined the board of Lincoln Electric Company in Cleveland, which made generators; then Banta, a printing, imaging, and supply chain corporation in Menasha, Wisconsin; followed by Dames and Moore, a civil engineering and construction company in California. And then American Express called. I sat on that board for fourteen years, until 2018.

One major board invitation often begets another, and I joined the board of Exxon Mobil Corporation in 2012 after being solicited for a few years by Rex Tillerson. I'd said no before to Rex because Xerox limited the number of boards that employees could sit on, and besides, I wasn't sure I wanted to serve on an energy company board. But as I thought about how vital energy is for prosperity and success throughout the world, I decided to get engaged. I am now board chair of Exxon's audit committee, which I happen to love. Audit is not the most sought-after committee because it can be boring and is quite a bit of work, but auditing is a necessary part of every organization, whether public, private, or nonprofit. Exxon is another great company, and the board is wonderful too.

I am often asked, especially by women, how to get on a board. I describe my path and advise them to start small with a position on a school board or the board of a local community organization or small company. Networking and developing and broadcasting their skills are also vital. Finally, having a reputation of working well with others is a top priority. But none of these suggestions are a guarantee. My first response to inquiries is to ask, "Do you know someone on a corporate board?" Then I ask, "What would the board gain from you being on it? What would you bring to the table?"

There are more women on major boards now than there were when I was coming up, when I was either the only woman or one of two, but we still have a long way to go. The Alliance for Board Diversity examined 1,033 new Fortune 500 board positions in 2018. They found that more than 80 percent were filled by whites, and of those new board members, 60 percent were men. Chief marketing officers are in demand, particularly those with digital marketing skills, as are female chief financial officers.

The big shift now is a greater demand for women and African Americans. As a result of the Me Too and Black Lives Matter movements, corporations are under either self-imposed or externally imposed pressure to diversify not only their management teams and employee base but also their boards. The murder of George Floyd escalated the steady drumbeat for diversity into a full-blown megaphone yell. Corporations are on the hotseat yet again to have their boards mirror the world's population. This is important because while the boards don't run the corporations, they set the tone and reflect what's important to them. They can force change. The boards have to approve executives' compensation and promotion paths.

Today, we're experiencing organized protest against the status quo. The light is shining on broad-based diversity of gender, race, sexual orientation, and ability. People believe, and rightfully so, that if a company has a diverse governance structure, then a diverse company will follow. And there is enormous pressure for change. I have received many calls from CEOs of public companies, small and large, asking for advice and board recommendations. I have also received calls from virtually every publication, including *The Wall Street Journal*, the *New York Times*, and *Fortune* magazine, as well as various television networks—Bloomberg, CNBC, CNN, BBC4—all asking about corporations' responsibility to meet the diversity challenge and to change their boardrooms. I help where I can, but I have a caution.

Some people may think that being on a board is all fun—even glamorous—and a windfall of money. They would be wrong. After you get over the headiness of being on a big board (or even a small one), the work begins. You have to be willing to dedicate the time, meeting five to seven times a year, not counting committee meetings. You won't be paid millions of dollars for your work. And the reputational risk is substantial. Boards and companies can be sued, for starters. Board members are generally personally protected by insurance, but every lawsuit or scandal takes up a lot of board time. Despite the drawbacks, serving on a board is worth it.

I was thrilled to have been invited to join the board of American Express so many years ago. It was the first charge card I'd ever owned, having applied for it in 1978 at a table the company had set up on the campus of Brooklyn Polytechnic. I had very little idea of how it worked. My mother only used cash, layaway, or food stamps for her purchases. She didn't even have a bank account. I had the card for at least a year before I used it for the first time; I bought a pair of shoes for $55 and paid off the entire amount when I got the bill. (I still do.) Credit was not something I was comfortable with. It was unheard of in my community to be able to have something for which you didn't have the money in your hand.

American Express took a gamble on me as a student, on all of us. I don't even know if they had the technology then to do a credit check; if they had, they would have found nothing. I literally had no credit history! Now they have ways to predict whether you are a good credit risk, and they make use of data and analytics that can predict your buying propensities and habits. The gathering of personal information has become an industry itself.

As I moved up the corporate ladder at Xerox, I began to transition from Ms. Inside to Ms. Outside. As head of BGO, I was asked to speak to various organizations as well as at important conferences. That led Anne to suggest I enlist the help of her speech coach, Ann Strianese, an independent contractor who coached Xerox executives. She was very good, unlike a few I'd worked with previously who tried to get me to speak differently, which caused me to lose interest and back away.

This speech coach was different. "How you sound is basically who you are," Ann said to me. "There's nothing we can do about that—it's just the way it is—so let's look at your content." The content she was referring to was in the talk I was about to give for the first time to our investors. She listened as I read the speech very quickly, which is the normal way I speak, without enunciating all the words and with the twang of New York City. She did not try to erase my accent, but she did get me to slow down and enunciate more clearly so at least the investors could understand my words. I had also used contractions like "it's" or "let's," and we substituted "it is" or "let us" because it forced me to slow down. She was really good.

She taught me that whatever story I had to tell had to include the facts, but from my point of view. That was critical for me. She understood that I took comfort in facts and that, for me to become a better, more comfortable speaker, I should center the speech around the facts. She also pointed out that I didn't have a good poker face. (Anne Mulcahy had said the same thing.) When someone asked a question, she said, the expression on my face immediately signaled whether I thought the question was stupid or smart. Sometimes you might want people to understand you're exasperated by the question, but there are other ways to get that across. You can, for example, reword the question so it becomes the one you want to answer. That saves you from projecting "That is the stupidest question I've ever heard."

How many times have I heard colleagues using "corporate speak," like when a corporate person responds to a question with big, meaningless phrases out of a business school manual? I couldn't do that. I learned to put my cards on the table from the get-go. My attitude was, "You can ask anything you want, but you have got to understand the three possible outcomes. One, I know the answer and am willing to tell you. Two, I know the answer and I'm not willing to tell you. And three, I don't know the answer, but I'll get back to you."

Some people, including journalists and analysts, persisted in asking the same question over and over after I'd refused to answer it the first time. I learned to fire back: "You can make my job really easy by repeatedly asking me the same question that I will not or cannot answer, or we can move on." Anne taught me a lot about situations like that, about feeling comfortable in my skin and focusing on the things that were important and not worrying about the bullshit stuff.

I wasn't the first at Xerox who sought out the help of a speech coach, or, more accurately, was advised to, but my work with Ann Strianese definitely helped. I worked off and on with her for many years. Other than the occasional two or three days I spent with her, I didn't have any continuous training at Xerox. Today, quite a few people have personal coaches. I did not.

Anne Mulcahy was my ultimate teacher. She was excellent and purposeful about grooming me and Jim Firestone, the chief strategist, and Armando Zagalo de Lima, the Portuguese head of European Operations, to make sure we all stayed focused on our current roles while preparing for larger roles. She taught me a hard lesson on leadership once when I was trying to persuade the vital head of developing markets (Latin America, Russia, and other emerging areas) not to leave the company.

It was a complicated negotiation. The head of developing markets had specific requests that were complicated because he was an expat and because he was paid in different currencies.

There was a bit of magic behind the deal between the company and this person. I didn't know the history when I was negotiating with him to stay at Xerox. He worked for me, and I spent a lot of time thinking up arrangements that would keep him with us. You can imagine my fury when he told me that he had already arranged the details with Anne. "Wait a minute. You don't work for Anne. You work for me," I said, erroneously thinking the arrangement with Anne had been made recently when, in fact, it had been made years before.

I was so hot under the collar that I called Anne and asked her, "Why did you agree to something with this guy behind my back?" Anne replied, "Whoa, whoa, what the hell are you talking about?" When I told her, she explained the timeline and reeled me back in. "Know what you're talking about before you call me," she said. "Clean it up a little bit. And let's not let ourselves get caught up in all these power plays. Let's start working on the problem." She was very good at turning things back toward what mattered. "First, get clarity on the problem and where the opportunities lie," she said, "and then we can start dealing with the personalities later."

That was one important lesson. Others followed. She called me out when I was stepping back too much or moving in too far or acting a little bit of an asshole. She was an amazing teacher. I admired her enormously for her competence in her own area, but she became a teacher in the things I was good at as well. She and I were so different in our approaches, yet we worked together as one.

My family was finally working together as well. My sister, who had been in and out of the criminal justice system on drug and petty crime charges and in and out of drug treatment programs, finally sobered up and stayed clean while I was head of the BGO. The finale began just before the Fourth of July holiday in 2004 while she was living with us in our wonderful house in Rochester. She had been arrested again, this time for shoplifting. Not wanting her to spend the long holiday weekend in jail, I turned to our local real estate lawyer, who managed to get her out. Lloyd and I had reached the end of our rope. Instead of taking her back into our home, we got her a room in a hotel in Rochester. "You stay there," I told her in a tough-love lesson. "Know that we are willing to help you when you're ready to actually deal with yourself, so call us. But moving you back into our house right now isn't going to work."

Our friend Linda Thornton Hillery, who had lost her sister to drug addiction, stepped up to the plate and saved us. She knew a judge and arranged for Deborah to be considered for the local drug court. This is a program for substance abusers who have been charged with nonviolent crimes and voluntarily enter the minimum year-long drug court program rather than go to jail. Deborah said later that when she saw the graduates at the drug court, she said, "This is what I want." Something clicked with my sister that day, and that was it. As of this writing, she has been sober for seventeen years and works in a chemical dependency agency in Rochester as an intake counselor.

I respect and admire my sister. She is the soul of our family, the one who remembers birthdays and anniversaries and who reminds me, when necessary, to be nice. My tendency to be blunt can sometimes offend people.

We were living a pretty normal family life in Rochester during my sister's recovery. Malcolm was about to go off to MIT, and Melissa attended high school at Allendale Columbia, a small, private, rigorous school less than a mile from our home. Melissa, a good student, needed the challenge because if she felt something wasn't worth her time, she had an unbelievable ability to just check out and daydream. She still does. She wasn't rude as a child or disobedient in the normal way, but she wasn't obedient either. She refused to participate in gym, for example, because her cousin Aja, who is seven years older, told her she didn't need gym to get into college and Melissa therefore saw it as of no use to her. Nothing would dissuade her. Malcolm, though technically my stepson, has been my child forever. We learned early on that he was dyslexic. We also learned that he was brilliant at math. He was a debater and argued his points to the end, which was sometimes exhausting.

We were a very vocal family. We argued and discussed and watched *Jeopardy*. My husband was definitely not ordinary. He had a scientist's brilliant mind but was not organized and sometimes drank too much. An unbelievably good cook, he would produce massive dinners most nights for all of us—standing rib roast, homemade mashed potatoes, rack of lamb with homemade mint jelly, acorn squash—and sometimes that was a success and sometimes it wasn't. There were times when Melissa just wanted to have pizza and go to her room.

We were four people with very different personalities living in one house with my sister living nearby, and we had to work it every day. Our life was filled with contrasts. One minute we were flying in a corporate jet or traveling Business or First Class on vacations that many families could not even conceive of, and the next minute we were fighting over who was going to clean up after dinner or—our biggest fight—take the garbage down our long driveway to the road. It was just unbelievable normality mixed with insane abnormality.

I was—and am—part of what I call the crossover generation. I was a first-generation executive. My husband was a first-generation executive. We had one foot in the white world and another in the Black world. We were both at the forefront of showing what it's like to participate from this new position for both the white people and the Black people. We had a very tight set of friends in Rochester, all of them African Americans we've known for years. They would come by on the weekends with their spouses and their kids for a summer barbeque or just to hang out. They didn't care about what I did at Xerox or what position I had. They accepted me for me. I had a social life independent of work, and I had a life at work. The two played different chords, but they played together in harmony.

Ironically, that harmony became strained in 2007—and with the least likely person, Anne Mulcahy—when I was appointed president of Xerox, chief operating officer, and member of the board. Anne and I had worked brilliantly together for years, dividing up problems, working independently in our different areas, piggybacking when it was called for. Now I was the heir apparent, and our relationship became a little confused.

This was more my problem than Anne's. I was moving toward "taking over" too quickly and showing impatience in meetings when Anne was giving advice about how to approach an issue. Anne was purposeful and clear when she addressed my disrespect for her position.

Fortune magazine ran a very good story about the impasse and our futile attempts to fit ourselves into the traditional order. It took a good dinner, with a good friend, to sort it out. Larry Zimmerman, whom Anne had persuaded a few years earlier to come out of retirement to be our CFO, pointed out that we were thinking too much about positioning ourselves and not enough about positioning Xerox for the future. He was right, of course. It would take the two of us, working in tandem as we had always done, to grow Xerox. So we forgot about checking the boxes on the organizational chart, and over time working together became natural again. We did earnings calls together. Anne covered strategy and the overall company, and I dove into the details of the areas I covered.

Being named president of Xerox had other repercussions beside my short-lived confusion with Anne. The appointment thrust me into the public eye as a curiosity on the one hand, and a sought-after oddity on the other. There was increasing pressure on corporations to diversify their leadership, and they got double marks with me. My new standing was driven not only by my position at Xerox but also by my reputation as a smart, firm, clear, and opinionated leader.

I received multiple invitations to speaking engagements, and I accepted as many as I possibly could. I wanted young women, especially young African American women, to see the possible result of years of hard work. They could look at me, a Black woman, and see themselves. I looked like them. I spoke like them. I had the same life references.

Getting to my new job presented its own challenges, as we still lived in Rochester but the corporate headquarters was in Norwalk, Connecticut. I also had a small apartment in New York City, and the first few months I was president I tried to live in the city and commute to Connecticut, but that didn't work well. The unpredictable traffic made it difficult to set a reasonable schedule. To arrive on time in the morning required leaving home far in advance, and the return trip could take over two hours. Back I went to Rochester. I would fly into Norwalk on Monday mornings and stay in a hotel or overnight at my place in New York. I finally bought a house in New Canaan, Connecticut, which became my home base. I thought my commute was tough, but it was run-of-the-mill compared to others'. Larry Zimmerman lived in Colorado and flew in every Monday. The company I joined after I retired from Xerox is based in Amsterdam, and every week one guy flew in from Norway and another from Switzerland. That's the way it works these days—or at least before the pandemic shut down airlines and closed borders, forcing people to work virtually.

My new position presented challenges of a different sort for my husband. I had to attend Xerox board meetings and dinners in New York City as well as American Express board meetings and other business events around the world. Earlier in my career, Lloyd would come to every event I'd asked him to and lend me his support and company, but after I became president and after he'd done everything once, he told me, "I'm not going. I don't serve any purpose there except to be your company." I understood entirely. He was certainly not your ordinary "trailing spouse." He didn't find those events stimulating or engaging. It was not the kind of thing he wanted to do, and I was fine with that.

I was insanely busy at work, beginning the long, perilous journey of seeing whether we could acquire ACS, being groomed by Anne on all aspects of the company for my eventual ascendance to CEO, being dispatched more and more by her to public events. I took over more responsibilities, I traveled with her more, and I did more of what she was doing. She even reestablished the role of president and used it as a training ground for me, enabling the rest of the organization to get comfortable with me as a leader. And through it all, the board was watching.

Anne was immensely generous during the transition. She sent me and my choice of colleagues to the White House in 2005 to receive the National Medal of Technology and Innovation from President Bush. "This is high ground," she told me. "You go take it." She sent me to that first lunch at the Obama White House with the other CEOs when I was still president. She sent me out into the world as the face of Xerox.

Another indicator of my impending appointment as CEO was an odd one. Xerox's legal department gave me a lengthy questionnaire to fill out to get security clearance from the US government. There were always two executives at Xerox who had security clearance, though you didn't know who they were. Xerox supplied all sorts of sensitive equipment and expertise to the government, like modifying our technology for use in submarines and on Air Force One. We also worked with the government on developing special machines that would wipe hard drives every thirty seconds and on testing specifications to prevent counterfeiting currency, like adding a gold strip to bills that could not be copied.

The security questionnaire was daunting. It required the dates of every single trip I'd ever been on outside the US, all the buildings I'd ever lived in and where I live now, and on and on. Fortunately, I had an administrative assistant who could fill in a lot of the information, but I had to go through a lot of old calendars. Then they wanted to know the names of my entire family—parents, aunts, uncles, kids, etc.—and my best friends and neighbors. I thought they were never going to follow up, but they did. Tony Raguasas, who lived across Greenfield Lane from us, called one day and asked, "Do you know I am being questioned about you by the FBI?" They called my brother, they called my good friend Linda Hillery. "Should I talk to them?" she asked me. Other people just talked to them without checking with me.

And then—nothing. No one notified me and said, "Congratulations, you have security clearance," or "Too bad, you failed." I had no idea until a year or two later when a few of my colleagues and I were invited to visit the Situation Room at the White House and I was able to skip the usual vetting process. "You can go right in," the presiding Marine said at the door. "You already have clearance."

Achieving the position of CEO was not as easy. The months and years stretched on, and while Anne and I worked seamlessly together—on the massive negotiations and renegotiations with

Fuji Xerox, on the acquisition of ACS—I began to get impatient. I was getting job inquiries from various companies, and though I never seriously considered leaving Xerox, the opportunities increased my impatience. I felt I was ready to run Xerox, and the inquiries reminded me that I wasn't CEO yet.

Sometimes my impatience got the better of me. I remember one highly charged meeting where I was preparing to present the company's quarterly earnings for the first time to the shareholders. This was a very important moment in the life of any publicly traded company, and for me. The audio of the presentation would be broadcast, and the results had to meet the formal requirements of the Securities and Exchange Commission. Just before I spoke, I spotted Anne in the room and I must have scowled at her, wanting that moment for myself, and she called me on it. "I could tell by your face that you didn't want me in the room, and everyone else could too," she scolded me afterward. "You'd better watch it. If you don't have the right level of respect and play your part for as long as it has to be played, you risk grabbing defeat from the jaws of victory. Right now, your part is that you're not the CEO. I am." She was right, of course, and I apologized.

It finally happened. Anne told me in June 2009 that my transition to CEO would take place in July. She later made the actual announcement to the Xerox family, and so it was that I became the first and, as of this writing eleven years later, the only Black woman to serve as the CEO of a Fortune 500 company.

AT THE HELM

My time as CEO was some of the best times that I had in my work life. The variability, complexity, and intensity of the role suited my personality well. Every day was different as I dealt with many multifaceted situations. In addition to expanding into services, Xerox had expanded distribution to small and midsize businesses through the acquisition of Global Imaging Systems (GIS) in April 2007. Global Imaging sold printers and copiers to small and midsize businesses. After the acquisition, GIS started selling Xerox products and services to their customer base. GIS continued to acquire independent dealers and expand distribution for Xerox. We continued this winning strategy throughout my time there. We also disposed of assets such as our information technology business by selling it to France's Atos in 2014. These types of transactions are complicated due to the legal, financial, and contractual elements but were common in my time as CEO as we continued to try to perfect our business mix and model.

I spent a significant amount of time meeting with employees, customers, suppliers, and partners around the world. These activities were some of the most important and enjoyable for me.

Employee meetings were a continuous and vital activity. Small meetings, including one-on-one meetings, and very large communication sessions were a normal part of my monthly calendar, and I realized that there was no substitution for face-to-face dialogue. I sent out many formal written communications as well as informal notes, but meeting personally with individuals was best for me. Back-and-forth, open and direct communication yields the best connection and imparts and gathers the best information. It also gave the employees and me a real human connection to one another and minimized misunderstandings.

At the start of every year, my leadership team and I held a kickoff event for the top two hundred to three hundred people in the company. We communicated how the company was doing as a whole—what was successful, what needed work—and recognized various types of success, including financial, social engagement, quality, leadership, and innovation. We also laid out the corporate strategy and plans for the year. This was a serious event that was action-filled. The top leaders were assigned work groups to develop and refine strategy, work on problems and opportunities, and meet and learn more about one another. Every evening we had dinner together, and the three-and-a-half-day event was capped with a big dinner. Some companies had lavish gatherings, taking over entire resorts in Florida or inviting everyone on a major cruise, but Xerox was not like that. We were more low-key and gathered near one of our factories or near a customer location. Serious work and fun.

Customer and vendor meetings were also a standard event—

three or four every month. Straight from the horse's mouth: how are we doing, what do you need, these are our plans, and on and on. No better way for me to spend my time. Most of these meetings were not drama- or issue-filled; their purpose was for us to learn, communicate, and build connections. At large customer or supplier sites I was sometimes asked to speak to the company's leadership team or employees. A typical visit was one that I made to Cisco Systems, a great customer and supplier to Xerox led by a great CEO, Chuck Robbins. I traveled to Cisco with the Xerox account executive, Suzi Good, and I was able to kill three birds with one stone—help sell a bit of Xerox's product and services, respond to a request from Chuck to speak to his company about transformation, and spend time with Xerox employees on the West Coast. Twenty-four hours in total. Connecticut to California. Five to six meetings. In and out, always moving.

Given the number of countries that Xerox operated in, the number of large customers and suppliers, and my belief that personal is best, it was inevitable that I racked up many, many flying miles and that my family saw little of me. I was in a cycle of high stress, little sleep, and less than ideal eating habits, but I loved every minute of it. Fortunately, a wake-up call came in the form of a health scare. In my first year, my friend Linda Hillery noticed a growth on my neck behind my ear. I had been moving so fast that I had not noticed it. Which was surprising, because it was not small. Though I needed a delicate and complicated surgery to remove the noncancerous tumor, the outcome was excellent, and my recovery was complete and not too long. I had to slow down, and I did for a while.

The board of directors, my bosses, were also a very important part of my responsibility and were very helpful to me. As chairwoman I convened the board meetings and was responsible for their content and for them running smoothly. I was able to recruit a few members to the board due to natural rotations, but the board was largely the same as when Anne was CEO. We met seven to eight times a year in scheduled day-and-a-half-long meetings. I also spoke to various members of the board on a regular basis. The board assured that Xerox had a viable strategy, had succession plans for key leadership positions, and remained financially viable and successful. The board kept and reported its financials to the appropriate standards. My team and I worked hard to keep the board well informed and involved in the business.

During my time as CEO, I also spent a lot of time in Washington, DC, and it taught me the importance of the constructive interaction between business and government. As I have already noted, I led President Obama's task force on STEM education, became a member of the BRT executive committee, served as the vice chair and then chair of the President's Export Council. I also worked on business issues specific to high technology companies as a member of and chair of the Technology CEO Council (TCC). I believe that this connection between government and industry is vital to the good functioning of business, the government, and society as a whole. I use the word "connection" for a reason—the relationship must be based on trust, an understanding of the roles and goals of each side, and a common view of the goals for the country. There are many places where the idea of a public/private partnership could result in a better outcome—education, trade, and immigration are a few examples. The goal is not for the government to implement whatever business wants, or vice versa. It is more to develop mutually acceptable policies that best serve the nation. This also holds true at the state level and internationally. Working toward a common goal is best.

Interestingly, the majority of my time as CEO was spent working the business. Pretty mundane: Digging into problems or opportunities and determining the appropriate approach and implementing it. How much and where should we invest our research dollars? Should we enter into joint development activities with universities, governments, or other companies? How should we "cover" the market from a selling perspective—should we continue to buy dealers to help sell to small and midsize businesses? What type and how much should we spend on marketing activities to assure the strong positioning of the company around the world? Do we have the correct talent and is it organized in the correct way? Succession plans for the executive team and key jobs like sales leaders, research lab managers, product development leads, as well as the company's performance and progress on diversity equity and inclusion were reviewed annually in a marathon three-to-four-day series of meetings. After a few years as CEO, I re-created my old role of executive assistant (EA) and hired a high-potential woman as my EA. She, along with my office support, was responsible for assuring that I used my time well, was prepared for the many, many meetings, and that I kept track of the actions and commitments that were made during external meetings. It was also a way for me to see a high-potential employee up close, and for her to get a glimpse into the executive level of the company. I had three EAs during my time as CEO, all diverse.

Xerox was going through significant transformation when I was at the helm, adding a diversified set of services from ACS. The business did not always go smoothly. The product business was performing well in a market that was under significant growth pressure caused by technology changes (less printing and more viewing) and competitive pressure. The services business results were mixed. Transportation services and document services were performing solidly but our digital health solutions business was struggling. ACS and then Xerox provided health solutions software to Alaska, New Hampshire, California, Texas, and others. These contracts were extremely complicated, and states had unique requirements. The theory of the case for this line of business was that Xerox would develop a standard software solution and deploy it with "minor" modifications to many states. The theory was not the reality. The standard solution never materialized as different states had specific requirements. At the end of the day this business was reduced significantly in the portfolio. But the amount of time, energy, and focus it took to come to a solution with and for the customers was a tremendous drain on the business.

All in all, Xerox was doing well in 2015; good but not great. The management team (with the board's agreement) was looking into additional ways to increase the company's value and return. Right around this time we were informed that we likely had an activist buying up our stock. Activists are shareholders who generally own between 5 and 10 percent of the shares in a company and have their own ideas about how the company should be run. Not all activists are bad; some can suggest appropriate ways for a company to make a bigger profit, but others can be very disruptive. Our activist shareholder turned out to be Carl Icahn, who had a reputation for being very difficult.

After a strategic review of the company's options, the management team and board decided to separate the company into two pieces: a focused BPO business that would build on its strong foundation, and a focused document technology business. This would give Xerox shareholders ownership in two businesses that were individually solid and had potential for value creation. This view of the business aligned with the view of Carl Icahn, but that did not drive our decision. The rest, as the saying goes, is history. In 2017, Xerox created two companies, Conduent and Xerox, and continued to struggle with the activist shareholder. But dealing with an activist, along with everything else, is all part of a day's work for a CEO.

When my daughter was younger, she asked, "Mom, what do you do or what did you do today?" I would tell her about my day, and her summary back to me was, "Oh, you go to meetings and travel." To the untrained eye her summary was correct. But in actuality what I did was listen, communicate, negotiate, enable, assist, build teams and businesses, and occasionally decide. I loved almost every minute of it.

PULLING BACK

There I was, at the height of my success, enjoying all the trappings of my position: money, access, a bully pulpit, respect. I had a great job and a great family. I also felt a bit of guilt—survivor's guilt. Why were there so few like me? So few Black or female or poor-beginnings people sitting around the table I had access to? I do know that I am not a unicorn by intelligence or endurance or education or sponsorship. My "uniqueness" shone a light on the grip that men, white men, have on the systems and institutions that they built. This was more obvious to me when I was named to the many "lists" published by *Fortune* and *TIME* magazine and others: "Most Powerful," "First Women Leaders," and so on. I was proud of these accomplishments and grateful, but I also realized that the criteria were indicative of the influence of the old white male establishment on the definitions and measures of success.

The traditional measure of power in business is the size of the organization you lead, how many people work for you, the amount of revenue your company generates, your personal earnings, and your company's market capitalization. (Market capitalization is the value of your company on the stock market.) Being recognized as a successful business leader is an important accomplishment, but it leaves out many other measures of accomplishment such as impacts on social justice, education, and the environment. The way I articulated it a few years ago was that my mother would never have made it onto any list, but nevertheless her impact on many people was profound. I believe that my mother's measure of success should be added to the business lexicon—leave behind more than you take away. This may be too simple, but we cherish and honor what we celebrate, and too often that's money and traditional power.

I also saw the power of access and, more important, the negative impact of lack of access. I was a poor kid with a determined mother who did not have access to anything but ambition for her children. The fact that we made it out of the housing projects to the greater world is attributable to her amazing resolve, helped by the social programs of the sixties and seventies. I was also assisted by the men, mostly white, at places like Brooklyn Polytechnic and Xerox who chose to take an interest in me. I was fortunate; others are not. Today, when poverty is demonized and poor schools, poor health care, and poor jobs are ignored, many more will be left behind and will never get out of their neighborhoods or their cycle of poverty. They and their families will remain trapped at the lowest echelon of society while those in the very exclusive, full-access, wealthy club remain at the top.

I worked hard and received an unbelievable amount of support and help, and I enjoyed the fruits of all of it. I do not believe in

socialist or communist systems in which resources are di[...]
evenly, independent of effort, education, or accomplishm[...]
also do not believe that the current version of American capitalism
is operating correctly. Equal opportunity requires that decent health
care, a good education, safe housing, and nutritious food must
be available to all. I believe business can and should play a more
direct role in this rebalancing of what is being called "inclusive
capitalism." We must have a society where a living wage, access to
affordable health care, training and retraining resources, child and
elder care, and environmental sustainability are part of the business
model. All this cannot be done by business alone. Businesses, governments, NGOs, and educational institutions must come together
in a new grand coalition that redefines US capitalism.

I have had the opportunity and good fortune to serve on the
boards of some of the leading nonbusiness organizations, including the Ford Foundation, the amazing social justice organization;
the Mayo Clinic, the leading health-care organization; and MIT,
the world-class institute of higher education with the mission to
help create a better world. I am often asked why I do this, why
I add more to my already full plate. This is the other side of the
scale: it keeps me balanced in some ways and keeps me sane. These
organizations are tackling some of the largest opportunities that
exist for a better society. They're doing it with optimism and hope,
and all I can do is lend my experience, effort, and brain to help.

I am not the only CEO engaged in these efforts—far from
it—which is why the public perception that corporate leaders,
especially CEOs, are focused only on their pockets and the bottom line is inaccurate. CEOs are paid very well, but they are as
motivated by their ability to build good, profitable, sustainable,

respected, and socially responsible companies as they are by their compensation.

I was really heartened in 2019, well after I retired from Xerox, to read that two hundred of my former CEO colleagues at the Business Roundtable had embraced and expanded the definition of corporate responsibilities. Now additional stakeholder issues will be given more weight, including the interests of employees (pay, benefits, training, diversity) and communities (community support, sustainability, environmental protection). This is a significant and responsible shift by the Business Roundtable given that every mission statement issued since 1997 had identified shareholder return as a CEO's and corporation's primary and sometimes only priority.

This is the first step in what is a hopeful time for business in America and around the world as economies recover from the pandemic and restructure. This type of effort, if diligently and carefully tackled, will do a lot to improve society's increasing distrust and disillusionment with business. The current interplay between society and business is extremely corrosive and damaging to democracy and capitalism. Businesses can—and do—contribute to the overall good. Demonizing business will do nothing but make it less responsive, less open, and less globally competitive.

I am also hopeful that this effort will improve the discourse regarding CEO compensation, especially in light of the wage stagnation that the average American worker has faced in the last few decades, which has been compounded by the unprecedented rate of unemployment driven by the pandemic. Wage stagnation is one of the cornerstones of the disillusionment that many Americans feel and is a failing of US capitalism. It is hard for many people to understand the numbers that are bandied around regarding CEO pay. When the *New York Times* or *The Wall Street Journal* reports that the compensation of the top CEOs is in the hundreds of millions of dollars, it is easy to understand why the average citizen doesn't like or trust corporate executives. As my friends say to me, "Who is worth that much money?" It is a good question.

Activist Carl Icahn's arrival at Xerox coincided with a pivotal time for me as I was actively laying out the next stages of my future. Xerox had been a core part of my life for the past thirty-six years, longer than I had known my husband. I had been with Xerox through the terms of six different US presidents, from the end of Jimmy Carter's administration to the beginning of Donald Trump's. A decision that could have been difficult for me was in fact easy to reach: the decision to step down.

A lot of factors led to my decision, but the primary one was my desire to spend more time with my husband. I was approaching sixty, and Lloyd was nearing eighty. He was in good health, but we'd had a terrible scare a few years before when one of his lungs collapsed. He'd been alone in the apartment in Rochester when it happened, and our dog saved his life by barking so long and so loud that the building manager came into the apartment and found him. Lloyd was very ill and had to have a portion of his lung removed. He was in the hospital for three long, worrying weeks. Vernon called me every single day to find out how I was doing. My husband had the best care in the world, Vernon said, but who was taking care of me? He was really great about it. But I realized that my husband and I were not playing to the best of us.

Lloyd's other lung wasn't in good shape either. The doctors didn't think he was strong enough to have both lungs operated on at the same time, so he had to go back in six months for a second surgery. He eventually recovered, but our life had to change. Who knew how much time we had left together?

As Lloyd approached his eightieth birthday, little was as it had been in our lives. The kids were grown and had moved out, Malcolm to California to attend Stanford, Melissa to NYU for her second master's. The company was evolving, an activist was in, and the country was changing under Trump in a devastating way.

It was not Trump's policies that I objected to, though I didn't like them, but his anti-American rhetoric toward people who had so much less. Racism and anti-Semitism were given a big boost after the white supremacist rally in Charlottesville, Virginia, during which a woman was killed and Trump famously said there were "very fine people on both sides." Muslims from seven countries were barred from entering the US, and Trump had declared Mexicans "murderers and rapists." Poor people were being punished for being poor, and their safety net was being whittled away. Lloyd and I were stunned. I had just enjoyed eight years of a president who didn't do everything perfectly but who, in fact, did many things right, and I liked and respected him as a human being. Now here was a man who had just been elected president of the United States who I did not respect at all. Lloyd and I started thinking about establishing an alternate residence in London. A new life without Xerox. A new life outside Trump's America.

Professionally, I was fulfilled at the top of Xerox, having been president and then CEO for nine years, the two roles being essentially the same. There was nowhere else to go in the company. Add to that the sheer number of years I'd worked at Xerox, which made my presence there seem routine. And last, the number of viable and interesting opportunities for me outside the company was increasing tenfold. You know you're nearing the end at one position when you start paying more attention to other opportunities and thinking, *Oh my god, I would be interested in doing that.* I was still young. I had lots of good years ahead of me.

I ran a good process within the company as I was transitioning Jeff Jacobson as the next CEO, making sure I had secured his number two team, the people who were going to lead, because with any transition there is a significant risk that many people will exercise their right and their ability to go elsewhere. I was dealing with the activist at the same time, and most of that occurred outside Jeff's view. We didn't know yet whether Icahn was going to insert himself into the management team, and the last thing I wanted was to contaminate Jeff with all the bullshit that has to go on with an activist. The good news was that I am comfortable with a fight, and that, basically, was what we had. I had the support of the board on our approach as well as much-needed expertise in activist response, including communications and strategy, all provided by Teneo, the CEO advisory firm. (I was so impressed with the work of Teneo that, after retirement, I became, and remain, a senior adviser there.) But I also knew that the longer I stayed at Xerox, the weaker my successor would be because the fight and the win would be mine and would therefore leave the next CEO vulnerable.

I officially retired as CEO of Xerox in December 2016. I had made it very clear that I wanted no party, no flowers, no present, nothing. I'd gotten a plaque of appreciation from the board of directors at the annual meeting for my seven years as CEO, and I'd received wonderful responses to my goodbye email to all 130,000-

plus employees in over 160 countries. Their messages meant way more to me than any ceremony. They were my going-away party.

I spent my final day packing up my office with my outstanding assistant, Rosemary Clark. I left behind everything I possibly could: the hundreds of engraved plexiglass awards Xerox or I had garnered during my thirty-six years at the company; the latest towering stack of business books I'd been sent by publishers and authors hoping for a jacket blurb or some sort of endorsement; my business files, reports, and memos. I am not a sentimental person, so there weren't a whole lot of boxes. My office was pretty bare to begin with. I traveled a lot for Xerox, and to me, my office was just somewhere to sit down and make phone calls and hold meetings when I was around.

The few things I did take meant something to me personally, especially the signed and framed certificate from President Obama appointing me as vice chair of the Export Council (I later became chair) and giving me a new title: The Honorable Ursula Burns. That was huge for me. Here was the first African American president of the United States honoring me, the first African American woman CEO of a Fortune 500 company. I had a picture from the ceremony with the president and my family at the White House, and I took that with me from my office as well.

I also took the engraved Lucite "headstone" I was given when I became president of Xerox and a member of the board in 2007 and an old, engraved clock commemorating the first big management job I'd headed twenty years before with the Office Products Technology Group, the guys who made fax machines. I'd given a congratulatory clock to everyone.

A few books went into the boxes. I took *Lean In* by Sheryl Sandberg, the COO of Facebook. I had talked to her about her book before it was published, and I liked it when I read it. I also took *Option B: Facing Adversity, Building Resilience, and Finding Joy*, which Sheryl had written after the sudden death of her husband, *Good to Great: Why Some Companies Make the Leap . . . and Others Don't* by Jim Collins because it was a good read, and both of Vernon Jordan's books, *Vernon Can Read* and *Make It Plain*, because Vernon is Vernon. The rest were consigned to what we called the Xerox Library, which meant the trash can. It was over. Almost.

I was going to stay on as chair of Xerox for six months, and that office was in the building next door. Barring any crisis, I would be out the door in June and ready to start a new life. There would still be quite a few Xerox obligations, of course. Programs and presentations had been planned years in advance, including my attending the America's Cup in Bermuda as a guest of Team Oracle. CEOs do not go quickly into that good night, but I went as fast as I could.

That might seem cold to some, but I have always been very project-oriented, and the Xerox project was over. I kept track of what was happening, of course, as Carl Icahn and another activist, Darwin Deason, the founder of ACS, continued to wreak havoc on the company, but I didn't interfere or offer advice to Jeff. The company was his to run, in his own way, and he had a good and strong board.

Xerox is a part of who I am. I loved it as I love my family—because it is family. My time there was very good for me and for the company, and I am proud of my contribution.

I had a sign hanging in my office: DON'T DO ANYTHING THAT WOULDN'T MAKE YOUR MOTHER PROUD. I think I honored that message along this journey. In fact, I'm sure of it.

AN END AND A BEGINNING

When I left Xerox, I received lots of advice about taking my time before getting involved in anything else. I always nodded and agreed that this was a smart idea. Well, I didn't do that because I didn't feel it. I retired from Xerox with no regrets, with the feeling that all was good, and I knew that I was not done. I was only done working for Xerox. I jumped right into another leadership role as the chairwoman of the board of Veon, a global telecom company with the goal of bringing world-class telecommunications and financial services to emerging markets like Bangladesh, Algeria, Russia, Ukraine, and Kazakhstan. When I joined the board, Veon was in a difficult place. It had weak leadership, a bloated and dysfunctional headquarters, and an inappropriate governance approach. In addition, years of underinvestment in the company was beginning to show. To top it all off, the company was under a deferred prosecution agreement and a federal monitorship imposed by US authorities for past corruption activities. My initial role as chair of the board at Veon unexpectedly expanded to executive chair and then chairwoman and CEO. The work was interesting, but it reminded me that I have a tendency to be over-busy, so after accomplishing my mission of remedying all of the above-mentioned issues, I left Veon after three years.

My husband and I split our time between New York City and London, where we bought a very nice flat in Battersea. I was still very involved in my board duties at Exxon Mobil. I'd retired from the Amex board in 2018 after ten years, and that same year I joined the boards at Nestlé and Uber. I kept the Ford Foundation, Mayo Clinic, and MIT. My passion for board service grows. It is the perfect after-work activity for me. And then I was faced with my biggest transition ever.

Lloyd died unexpectedly in January 2019. A shock. A disaster. I could not deal with it. Lloyd was my absolute everything; I just didn't realize how much this was true. I was totally lost, sad, angry, guilty, and more. I loved Lloyd so much, even though, after thirty years, our relationship might have appeared to others to be habitual—always there, nothing exciting. Exactly. That is exactly what I miss. I hadn't realized how dependent I was on my family, especially my husband. Eighteen months later, I still have an ache in my heart.

What I came to realize in the last year is what most people realize during their bereavement: life goes on. In reality, mine is not a melancholy life. After a year and a half, I'm more happy than sad; I'm strong and rebuilding a fulfilling new life.

It is hard for me to explain Lloyd to anyone without using the words "crazy" and "great." He was a difficult man to get hold of: dyslexic, a brilliant scientist, very disorganized, a bit of a drinker, a terrible communicator, not a saint or saintly, but with a pure and unbelievably gentle and caring heart. All in all, perfect. I absolutely would not have made it or been happy without him, and I still hate the fact that he has left us, left me. He continues to be the wind beneath my wings. I wake up every day and miss him, and I go to sleep most nights thinking about him. I believe there is life after death: it's in the people you leave behind.

I absolutely love and appreciate my country—a land of immigrants who often come with nothing but their hopes and dreams. They work hard, invest in their families, and move up over generations. That is essentially my story, but division, negative discourse, hate, racism, and sexism are working today to undermine everything that America has stood for. Despite the dark days we are in as I write this, I am optimistic about the future, probably because I am a bit naive. America is scrappy and has come through difficult times—slavery, civil war, Vietnam, 9/11—and pulled together. I will continue to work for the more perfect union.

I am blessed with the best friends in the world. They keep me happy, supported, real, protected, and energized. My close friends are regular "sisters" (and several men) I have known for years. We are a team. The interesting thing is that none of my sisters are corporate types, none are rich—not even close. Deborah, Catherine (and her husband, Hamish), Linda, Antoinette, Vickie, Suzi, Deborah (and her husband, Jim), and others keep me going, as well as my men friends: Vernon, Darren, Tim, Michael and Eric, Declan, and Mercer, among others. There is a saying that friendship is the fruit of life, and that is absolutely true in my case.

I am also blessed to call so many young people my friends, my kids, Melissa and Malcolm, as well as my nieces, Tara and Terri, my granddaughter, Aja, and her husband, Andreas, and other young people like Sarah, James, Olivia, Justin, Q'uran, Devin, Tiffany, and Krystal. It is quite amazing how different their lives are from my generation's. Technology, social progress or lack thereof, and global travel have thrust these young people to the forefront of social and business change, but despite this I know that my mother's instructions are more applicable for them than they were for my generation.

Leave behind more than you take away.

Don't let the world happen to you. You happen to the world.

God doesn't like ugly.

Take care of each other.

Don't do anything that wouldn't make your mother proud.

Where you are is not who you are (and remember that when you're rich and famous).

ACKNOWLEDGMENTS

This book would not have been possible without Linda Bird Francke, who helped me every step of the journey. Distance, shutdown, and personal challenges on both sides were no match to the Francke/Burns team—thanks almost entirely to Linda.

Thanks to Lynn Nesbit, my agent; to Declan Kelly, CEO of Teneo, for the connections to the agent, publisher, and lawyers; and to my personal lawyers, Michael Aiello and Michael Epstein of Weil, Gotshal & Manges LLP.

Thanks to the amazing team at HarperCollins: Tracy Sherrod, editor par excellence; Judith Riotto, my copy editor; and Trina Hunn, in legal, for reading this manuscript with their expert eyes.

Vernon Jordan; Wayland Hicks; Catherine Cronin; my brother and sister, Terry Burns and Deborah Eastman; my cousin Napoleon; and others suffered through interviews and questions.

Without Xerox historic records I would be lost.

Thanks to my kids, Melissa and Malcolm, for continuous and varying contributions (like fact-checking and family memory) throughout the writing process.

ABOUT THE AUTHOR

Ursula M. Burns is an American businesswoman. She is currently senior adviser of Teneo and serves on the board of directors of Uber, Exxon Mobil, Nestlé, Waystar, and IHS Holding. She also serves on the board of the Ford Foundation, Mayo Clinic, and MIT, as well as other nonprofit organizations. She was the chairwoman of Veon Ltd. from 2017 to 2020 and CEO from 2018 until 2020. She served as CEO of Xerox from 2009 to 2016 and as chairwoman from 2010 to 2017. She regularly appeared on *Forbes*'s and *Fortune*'s most-powerful-woman lists. She was a leader of the STEM program of the Obama White House from 2009 to 2016, and vice chair of the President's Export Council from 2010 until 2015 and then chair of the President's Export Council from 2015 to 2016. She lives in London and in New York.